P9-CDB-089

Lee Trevino

CEDAR PARK CHRISTIAN SCHOOL
HIGH SCHOOL LIBRARY
16300 112th Ave. N.E.
Bothell, WA 98011

Consulting Editors

Rodolfo Cardona
professor of Spanish
and comparative literature,
Boston University

James Cockcroft
visiting professor of Latin American
and Caribbean studies,
State University of New York at Albany

Hispanics of Achievement

Lee Trevino

Thomas W. Gilbert

Chelsea House Publishers
New York   Philadelphia

CHELSEA HOUSE PUBLISHERS

Editor-in-Chief: Remmel Nunn
Managing Editor: Karyn Gullen Browne
Copy Chief: Mark Rifkin
Picture Editor: Adrian G. Allen
Art Director: Maria Epes
Assistant Art Director: Noreen Romano
Manufacturing Manager: Gerald Levine
Systems Manager: Lindsey Ottman
Production Manager: Joseph Romano
Production Coordinator: Marie Claire Cebrián

Hispanics of Achievement
Senior Editor: John W. Selfridge

Staff for LEE TREVINO
Associate Editor: Philip Koslow
Copy Editor: Joseph Roman
Designer: Robert Yaffe
Editorial Assistant: Martin Mooney
Picture Researcher: Nisa Rauschenberg
Cover Illustration: Bruce Weinstock

Copyright © 1992 by Chelsea House Publishers, a division of Main
Line Book Co. All rights reserved. Printed and bound in the
United States of America.

First Printing

1 3 5 7 9 8 6 4 2

Library of Congress Cataloging-in-Publication Data
Gilbert, Tom
  Lee Trevino/Tom Gilbert
    p. cm.—(Hispanics of achievement)
  Includes bibliographical references and index.
  Summary: A Biography of the acclaimed Mexican American golfer
  ISBN 0-7910-1256-5
    0-7910-1283-2 (pbk.)
  1. Trevino, Lee—Juvenile literature. 2. Golfers—United States—
Biography—Juvenile literature. 3. Hispanic Americans—Biog-
raphy—Juvenile literature. [1. Trevino, Lee. 2. Golfers. 3. Mexican
Americans—Biography.] I. Title. II. Series.
GV964.T73G55 1991   91-2880
796.352'092—dc20   CIP
  [B]   AC

Table of Contents

Hispanics of Achievement

Oscar Arias Sánchez
Costa Rican president

Joan Baez
Mexican-American folksinger

Rubén Blades
Panamanian lawyer and entertainer

Jorge Luis Borges
Argentine writer

Juan Carlos
King of Spain

Pablo Casals
Spanish cellist and conductor

Miguel de Cervantes
Spanish writer

Cesar Chavez
Mexican-American labor leader

El Cid
Spanish military leader

Roberto Clemente
Puerto Rican baseball player

Plácido Domingo
Spanish singer

El Greco
Spanish artist

Gloria Estefan
Cuban-American singer

Gabriel García Márquez
Colombian writer

Raul Julia
Puerto Rican actor

José Martí
Cuban revolutionary and poet

Rita Moreno
Puerto Rican singer and actress

Pablo Neruda
Chilean poet and diplomat

Antonia Novello
U.S. surgeon general

Octavio Paz
Mexican poet and critic

Javier Pérez de Cuéllar
Peruvian diplomat

Anthony Quinn
Mexican-American actor

Diego Rivera
Mexican artist

Linda Ronstadt
Mexican-American singer

Antonio López de Santa Anna
Mexican general and politician

George Santayana
Spanish poet and philosopher

Junípero Serra
Spanish missionary and explorer

Lee Trevino
Mexican-American golfer

Pancho Villa
Mexican revolutionary

CHELSEA HOUSE PUBLISHERS

INTRODUCTION

Hispanics of Achievement

Rodolfo Cardona

The Spanish language and many other elements of Spanish culture are present in the United States today and have been since the country's earliest beginnings. Some of these elements have come directly from the Iberian Peninsula; others have come indirectly, by way of Mexico, the Caribbean basin, and the countries of Central and South America.

Spanish culture has influenced America in many subtle ways, and consequently many Americans remain relatively unaware of the extent of its impact. The vast majority of them recognize the influence of Spanish culture in America, but they often do not realize the great importance and long history of that influence. This is partly because Americans have tended to judge the Hispanic influence in the United States in statistical terms rather than to look closely at the ways in which individual Hispanics have profoundly affected American culture. For this reason, it is fitting

that Americans obtain more than a passing acquaintance with the
origins of these Spanish cultural elements and gain an under-
standing of how they have been woven into the fabric of American
society.

It is well documented that Spanish seafarers were the first to
explore and colonize many of the early territories of what is today
called the United States of America. For this reason, students of
geography discover Hispanic names all over the map of the United
States. For instance, the Strait of Juan de Fuca was named after
the Spanish explorer who first navigated the waters of the Pacific
Northwest; the names of states such as Arizona (arid zone), Mon-
tana (mountain), Florida (thus named because it was reached on
Easter Sunday, which in Spanish is called the feast of Pascua
Florida), and California (named after a fictitious land in one of the
first and probably the most popular among the Spanish novels of
chivalry, *Amadis of Gaul*) are all derived from Spanish; and there
are numerous mountains, rivers, canyons, towns, and cities with
Spanish names throughout the United States.

Not only explorers but many other illustrious figures in Spanish
history have helped define American culture. For example, the
13th-century king of Spain, Alfonso X, also known as the Learned,
may be unknown to the majority of Americans, but his work on the
codification of Spanish law has greatly influenced the evolution
of American law, particularly in the jurisdictions of the Southwest.
For this contribution a statue of him stands in the rotunda of the
Capitol in Washington, D.C. Likewise, the name Diego Rivera may
be unfamiliar to most Americans, but this Mexican painter influenced many American artists whose paintings, commissioned
during the Great Depression and the New Deal era of the 1930s,
adorn the walls of government buildings throughout the United
States. In recent years the contributions of Puerto Ricans,
Mexicans, Mexican Americans (Chicanos), and Cubans in
American cities such as Boston, Chicago, Los Angeles, Miami,
Minneapolis, New York, and San Antonio have been enormous.

The importance of the Spanish language in this vast cultural complex cannot be overstated. Spanish, after all, is second only to English as the most widely spoken of Western languages within the United States as well as in the entire world. The popularity of the Spanish language in America has a long history.

In addition to Spanish exploration of the New World, the great Spanish literary tradition served as a vehicle for bringing the language and culture to America. Interest in Spanish literature in America began when English immigrants brought with them translations of Spanish masterpieces of the Golden Age. As early as 1683, private libraries in Philadelphia and Boston contained copies of the first picaresque novel, *Lazarillo de Tormes*, translations of Francisco de Quevedo's *Los Sueños*, and copies of the immortal epic of reality and illusion *Don Quixote*, by the great Spanish writer Miguel de Cervantes. It would not be surprising if Cotton Mather, the arch-Puritan, read *Don Quixote* in its original Spanish, if only to enrich his vocabulary in preparation for his writing *La fe del cristiano en 24 artículos de la Institución de Cristo, enviada a los españoles para que abran sus ojos* (The Christian's Faith in 24 Articles of the Institution of Christ, Sent to the Spaniards to Open Their Eyes), published in Boston in 1699.

Over the years, Spanish authors and their works have had a vast influence on American literature—from Washington Irving, John Steinbeck, and Ernest Hemingway in the novel to Henry Wadsworth Longfellow and Archibald MacLeish in poetry. Such important American writers as James Fenimore Cooper, Edgar Allan Poe, Walt Whitman, Mark Twain, and Herman Melville all owe a sizable debt to the Spanish literary tradition. Some writers, such as Willa Cather and Maxwell Anderson, who explored Spanish themes they came into contact with in the American Southwest and Mexico, were influenced less directly but no less profoundly.

Important contributions to a knowledge of Spanish culture in the United States were also made by many lesser known individuals—teachers, publishers, historians, entrepreneurs, and others—with a love for Spanish culture. One of the most significant of these contributions was made by Abiel Smith, a Harvard College graduate of the class of 1764, when he bequeathed stock worth $20,000 to Harvard for the support of a professor of French and Spanish. By 1819 this endowment had produced enough income to appoint a professor, and the philologist and humanist George Ticknor became the first holder of the Abiel Smith Chair, which was the very first endowed Chair at Harvard University. Other illustrious holders of the Smith Chair would include the poets Henry Wadsworth Longfellow and James Russell Lowell.

A highly respected teacher and scholar, Ticknor was also a collector of Spanish books, and as such he made a very special contribution to America's knowledge of Spanish culture. He was instrumental in amassing for Harvard libraries one of the first and most impressive collections of Spanish books in the United States. He also had a valuable personal collection of Spanish books and manuscripts, which he bequeathed to the Boston Public Library.

With the creation of the Abiel Smith Chair, Spanish language and literature courses became part of the curriculum at Harvard, which also went on to become the first American university to offer graduate studies in Romance languages. Other colleges and universities throughout the United States gradually followed Harvard's example, and today Spanish language and culture may be studied at most American institutions of higher learning.

No discussion of the Spanish influence in the United States, however brief, would be complete without a mention of the Spanish influence on art. Important American artists such as John Singer Sargent, James A. M. Whistler, Thomas Eakins, and Mary Cassatt all explored Spanish subjects and experimented with Spanish techniques. Virtually every serious American artist living today has studied the work of the Spanish masters as well as the great 20th-century Spanish painters Salvador Dalí, Joan Miró, and Pablo Picasso.

The most pervasive Spanish influence in America, however, has probably been in music. Compositions such as Leonard Bernstein's *West Side Story*, the Latinization of William Shakespeare's *Romeo and Juliet* set in New York's Puerto Rican quarter, and Aaron Copland's *Salon Mexico* are two obvious examples. In general, one can hear the influence of Latin rhythms—from tango to mambo, from guaracha to salsa—in virtually every form of American music.

This series of biographies, which Chelsea House has published under the general title HISPANICS OF ACHIEVEMENT, constitutes further recognition of—and a renewed effort to bring forth to the consciousness of America's young people—the contributions that Hispanic people have made not only in the United States but throughout the civilized world. The men and women who are featured in this series have attained a high level of accomplishment in their respective fields of endeavor and have made a permanent mark on American society.

The title of this series must be understood in its broadest possible sense: The term *Hispanics* is intended to include Spaniards, Spanish Americans, and individuals from many countries whose language and culture have either direct or indirect Spanish origins. The names of many of the people included in this series will be immediately familiar; others will be less recognizable. All, however, have attained recognition within their own countries, and often their fame has transcended their borders.

The series HISPANICS OF ACHIEVEMENT thus addresses the attainments and struggles of Hispanic people in the United States and seeks to tell the stories of individuals whose personal and professional lives in some way reflect the larger Hispanic experience. These stories are exemplary of what human beings can accomplish, often against daunting odds and by extraordinary personal sacrifice, where there is conviction and determination. Fray Junípero Serra, the 18th-century Spanish Franciscan missionary, is one such individual. Although in very poor health, he devoted the last 15 years of his life to the foundation of missions throughout California—then a mostly unsettled expanse of land— in an effort to bring a better life to Native Americans through the cultivation of crafts and animal husbandry. An example from recent times, the Mexican-American labor leader Cesar Chavez has battled bitter opposition and made untold personal sacrifices in his effort to help poor agricultural workers who have been exploited for decades on farms throughout the Southwest.

The talent with which each one of these men and women may have been endowed required dedication and hard work to develop and become fully realized. Many of them have enjoyed rewards for their efforts during their own lifetime, whereas others have died poor and unrecognized. For some it took a long time to achieve their goals, for others success came at an early age, and for still others the struggle continues. All of them, however, stand out as people whose lives have made a difference, whose achievements we need to recognize today and should continue to honor in the future.

Lee Trevino

Lee Trevino, sporting a golf cap with his sombrero logo on it, smiles for a photographer during the 1978 U.S. Open.

CHAPTER ONE

Buying the Alamo

It was a June morning in 1968. A hazy midsummer sun hung in the sky over Oak Hill Country Club in Rochester, New York, where the United States Golf Association (USGA) was preparing to kick off the 68th edition of its prestigious annual championship—the U.S. Open. Oak Hill's beautiful 6,962-yard East Course was freshly manicured. Already known as a demanding course, it was expected to be a fitting arena for the elite of the world's professional golfers, who had assembled to compete for the title of U.S. Open champion and for $30,000 in first-prize money.

The thousands of spectators gathered at the scene and the millions of fans who were watching the event on television were also ready. The galleries were full, and the television cameras were in place, prepared to follow the action from the first hole to the 18th. All were looking forward to more of the classic confrontations that had long characterized America's oldest golf tournament. Along with the British Open, the PGA (Professional Golfers Association) Championship, and the Masters, the U.S. Open is one of the four

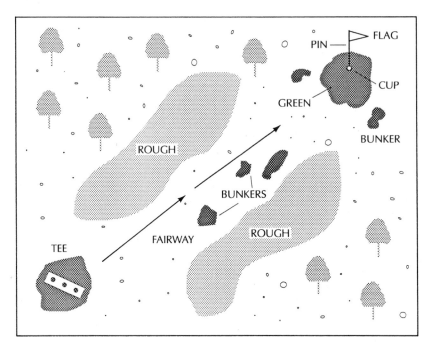

A diagram of the first hole at the Olympic Club in San Francisco, California, where Trevino made his U.S. Open debut in 1966. Unaccustomed to the high roughs and difficult bunkers (sand traps) of the Olympic course, Trevino finished 54th and came away with only $600. Two years later, he was the Open champion.

paramount golf events in the world, with a tradition going back to 1895. Its champions had included greats from every era—Harry Vardon, Willie Anderson, Francis Ouimet, Walter Hagen, Bobby Jones, Ben Hogan, and more recently Jack Nicklaus and Arnold Palmer. The conservative, almost machinelike Nicklaus was already a two-time U.S. Open winner and the defending champion; Palmer, a crowd-pleasing all-out competitor, had won the Open in 1960 and had dueled Nicklaus to the finish in 1967.

As it turned out, those who were hoping to see history made at Oak Hill got what they came for. They saw the 1968 U.S. Open champion come from behind to shoot 275 over 4 rounds—tying the U.S. Open record set the previous year—and finish 5 strokes ahead of the field. The champion, however, was not named Nicklaus or Palmer. Much to everyone's surprise, neither of golf's two dominant figures played well enough to be a real factor. The tournament came down to a stirring duel between Bert Yancey, a second-rank tour veteran who had yet to win a major championship, and a complete unknown named Lee Trevino, who was playing in only his first full season on the tour.

With few other well-known golfers playing well, Yancey was the story in the early going. A tall, blond 29 year old from suburban Radnor, Pennsylvania, who had attended the U.S. Military Academy, Yancey radiated cool professionalism and self-control as he shot 67 and 68, taking a 2-stroke lead at the halfway point. The lead appeared to be a commanding one in that Yancey's strongest competition was the inexperienced Trevino. As Trevino later remembered, "I believe that in his heart Yancey thought he had it won because I was the only person giving him any heat. Nicklaus was five shots behind me."

Trevino continued to hang tough through the third round, turning in a 69 to Yancey's 70 and closing to within 1 stroke. Both men were on record paces; Trevino's 206 had tied the U.S. Open's 3-round record score, and Yancey's 205 had broken it. Much was made in the press about the many contrasts, both on and off the course, offered by the two men. Besides his status as a veteran and his classic all-American looks, Yancey's style was utterly orthodox, right down to the smooth, even rhythm of his play and his graceful, deep swing. By contrast, Trevino was a short, thickly built Mexican American with a jaunty manner. Trevino's origins could not have resembled Yancey's less. Trevino came from the wrong side of the tracks, both socially and professionally. A desperately poor boy who never knew his father, he had been raised in a run-down house on the outskirts of Dallas, Texas, by his mother, who worked as a maid, and his hard-drinking Mexican-born grandfather, a gravedigger.

18

Trevino celebrates as he sinks a 20-foot birdie putt during the final round of the 1968 U.S. Open. He finished the round with a 69, 3 under par, and became the only man in the history of the Open to shoot below 70 in all 4 rounds.

It was only by a series of chance occurrences and lucky breaks that Trevino's natural athletic talent was able to develop. Whereas most golfers on the contemporary PGA scene could trace their origins in the sport to membership in a private country club or to a relative who was a golf enthusiast, Trevino got his start by shagging stray golf balls for pocket change at a public course that happened to be located close to where he lived; later, he worked his way up to a job as a caddie.

Caddying allowed him lots of free practice time, and in his teens he soon became a local golfing sensation around the Dallas area. As a young man, Trevino found that there was money to be made in golf from betting and, as was often true in his case, having other people bet on him. Under the guidance of various professional gamblers and wealthy sponsors, he managed to support his family. In his early twenties, the last place Trevino's career seemed likely to be heading was the PGA Tour.

Adding to the overall impression that Trevino was, as the *Sporting News* put it, a "reformed hustler" was his odd-looking technique. Being almost completely self-taught, he had developed an unusually flat swing that looked more suited to baseball than to golf. Though in later years he pointed out quite correctly that hitting the ball well time after time is more important than having picture-perfect form, during the Open he was inclined to play up his lack of polish. "I've got a bad swing," he told reporters, "probably the worst on the tour. I guess I don't swing at all. I move forward on the ball and kinda lunge at it. It must look like a caveman killing his lunch."

In fact, Trevino was thoroughly relishing the underdog role. As he later recalled in his 1982 autobiography, *They Call Me SuperMex*, Trevino felt that all the pressure was on his opponent: "I knew I could shoot 80 and nobody would be surprised, but if I played well it put pressure on Yancey, who was expected to win. I liked my position."

Yancey and Trevino were paired in a twosome for the final round. Trevino, wearing red socks to go with his red shirt and black trousers—not the most classic golfing attire—gave his rival some encouragement by mishitting his opening drive and finishing at one over par—a bogey, in golf terms—for the first hole. (Par, varying from 3 to 5 over the 18 holes of a golf course, is the number of strokes a golfer is expected to use in getting the ball from the tee into the cup—par for the course is normally 72.) But the much-anticipated duel between the two top contenders failed to materialize. After watching Yancey turn in a bogey of his own on the ninth hole, Trevino seized a one-stroke lead; from that point on he never looked back. He scored a birdie—one under par—on the 11th hole with a 30-foot putt and birdied 12 with a difficult uphill 20-footer. While playing the long par-5 13th hole, Trevino walked over to Joe Dey, the USGA's executive director, slapped him on the back, and said in a loud voice, "I'm just trying to build up as big a lead as I can, so I won't choke." In the future, Trevino's fans would learn to recognize that kind of talk as a sign of supreme confidence; he was beginning to smell the first great victory of his professional career.

Perhaps a little in shock to find himself holding a 5-shot advantage on his way to the 14th hole while being serenaded with cries of *¡Olé!* from the gallery, Trevino began to play as if he were

Trevino consoles Jack Nicklaus after the 1968 U.S. Open. Nicklaus, the 1967 champion and the dominant player on the PGA Tour, was the favorite at Oak Hill. By the third round, however, the battle for golf's most prestigious trophy was being waged by Trevino and Bert Yancey.

disconcerted by the sudden transformation from underdog to front-runner. In trouble on 14, 15, and 16, he scrambled to record unimpressive pars. Playing the 17th hole, Trevino disagreed with his caddie, Kevin Quinn, over whether to use a 1-iron or a 2-iron for his second shot. Trevino went with the 2-iron against his better judgment and topped the ball; it came to rest well short of the hole. As he had on so many of the previous holes, Trevino again had to scramble to make par. (After his victory, Trevino gave Quinn a $2,000 tip and stated that he would never have won the Open without the caddie's advice and support.)

On the final hole, and in a situation where most golfers would be thinking only of playing it safe, Trevino was no longer remotely concerned with his margin of victory over the quickly fading Yancey; he was aiming to break Jack Nicklaus's U.S. Open record total of 275. Deciding to go for broke, Trevino overdid it and hooked his drive into the rough on the left-hand side of the fairway. "When I found the ball," he said afterward, "it was deeply buried. I thought about chipping back to the fairway, but what kind of a finish is that for the Open champion to make?" Using a 6-iron, he got into more trouble on his next shot, which landed in another rough area on the edge of a slope some 100 yards from the flag. Trusting in his feeling that he had been hot all afternoon, Trevino took out his sand wedge and swung hard. The ball carried out of the tall grass, sailed high into the air, and came to rest a mere three feet from the cup. ("If you or I had had to play Trevino's third shot," reflected the veteran golf writer Herbert Warren Wind, "we would have been lucky to chop the ball halfway to the green, but he made contact with the ball so precisely and smoothly that it looked as if it had been sitting on a hairbrush.") With his next and 275th stroke of the tournament, Trevino parred the 18th hole. Even if he had to settle for tying the Open record, Trevino could be proud of being the only man in U.S. Open history ever to shoot below 70 in all 4 rounds. As for Yancey, he finished with a 76 and slipped into third place behind Nicklaus.

Arnold Palmer lines up a putt during a 1964 tournament while some of his adoring fans, known as Arnie's Army, look on. Palmer played Oak Hill with his usual power and aggressiveness, but the course had been designed to favor the accuracy and finesse that were Trevino's trademarks.

If Trevino had been taken lightly by the golf world before the Open, his dramatic victory made little difference, at least in the short term. *Impossible* and *fluke* were two of the words most commonly used by headline writers reporting Trevino's victory. Trevino's unconventional appearance and manner, his funny swing, his humble background and Mexican ancestry may all have caused people to doubt the ability he had just demonstrated on the golf course.

Since golf became popular in the United States during the 1890s, it has appealed mainly to a white middle-class segment of society. Not surprisingly, the game as a whole has tended to reflect the attitudes and values of the group that supports it. Although professional golf has become racially integrated, the golfing establishment has always practiced a subtler brand of racial and ethnic exclusion than has baseball or the other major sports. In 1990, 40 years after Charlie Sifford was grudgingly allowed to become the first black on the pro tour, reports of discrimination by prominent golf clubs were featured on the nation's sports pages. The Shoal Creek Club in Birmingham, Alabama, slated to host the 1990 PGA Championship, made headlines when its president announced that the club would never admit blacks. After several major corporations withdrew their sponsorship of the tournament, however, Shoal Creek did a quick about-face and invited a prominent black banker to become a member. Later in the year, the big-name golfer Tom Watson resigned his membership at the Kansas City Country Club when the club rejected the application of a prominent Jewish businessman. (Following the Shoal Creek controversy, the PGA issued guidelines for all clubs hosting its events, requiring evidence that the clubs were seeking members from minority groups.) In 1968, the golf world was simply not prepared to see a Mexican American from an impoverished background clutching its most prestigious trophy.

But the main cause of the doubts about Trevino was his lack of experience in big-time events. He may have been 28 years old and full of confidence, but his rise from anonymity to stardom had started only as recently as 1967, barely 12 months before his U.S. Open championship.

In late 1966, when Trevino was employed as the golf pro at a country club in El Paso, Texas, called Horizon Hills, he entered the U.S. Open at San Francisco's Olympic Club. His entire professional résumé up to that point consisted of a second-place finish in the 1965 Mexican Open, Texas Open victories in 1965 and 1966, and fifth place in the 1966 Panama Open. Discouraged by the tree-lined Olympic course, with its lush roughs and undulating fairways—so different from the flat, open courses of Texas—he played very poorly and came in tied for 54th place. His share of the winnings came to $600.

Runner-up Bert Yancey congratulates Trevino at the finish of the 1968 U.S. Open. The drama of the final round was heightened by the contrast between the tall, blond Yancey, a former West Point cadet, and the stocky Mexican American from the wrong side of the tracks.

After the Open, a dejected Trevino returned to the two-room Horizon Hills apartment that he shared with his wife, Claudia, and his baby daughter, Leslie. "The way my life was going at that time," he recalled, "if I had had a pumpkin patch, they would've canceled Halloween." The following year, when the USGA sent him an entry form for the 1967 U.S. Open at Baltusrol Golf Club in Springfield, New Jersey, he did not even bother to open the envelope. Claudia Trevino took it upon herself to scrape together the entry fee and send in the form on her husband's behalf. Trevino reluctantly agreed to take his chances in the rigorous 72-hole qualifying process. He managed to qualify, and armed with a small suitcase, a bag containing 12 golf clubs, and an airline ticket paid for by friends,

Trevino arrived in New Jersey as a complete unknown. Put off by the formal atmosphere of the stately old Baltusrol clubhouse, he divided his time between the low-budget highway motel where he was staying and a nearby Chinese restaurant. Trevino spent a week of lonely evenings and nights. He was itching to get back on the golf course each day, and his score showed it; he shot an excellent 280 in 4 practice rounds. He then caused a minor sensation by nearly repeating the feat in the actual competition, shooting 283 to finish in fifth place, only 8 strokes back of winner Jack Nicklaus. As soon as the competition had ended, he ran to telephone his wife with the news that they were now rich. "I'm not believing this," he blurted out. "I just won $6,000!"

Veteran observers of the golf scene were less impressed; they had seen countless unknown pros get hot during a big tournament and then just as suddenly return to obscurity forever. But Trevino did not fade away. He competed in 14 PGA Tour events in 1967 and won almost $30,000. That was a very respectable annual total for the time, no matter how small it might seem compared to the earnings of big-name golfers in the 1980s and 1990s. "How long has this been going on?" a smiling Trevino wisecracked as he followed up on his 1967 promise by earning over $50,000 on his first 17 tour stops in 1968. Although he had not yet won a major tournament, Trevino was building up a head of steam. By June, he was ready for Oak Hill.

After he had completed the 18th hole of his dramatic runaway victory in Round 4 of the 1968 U.S. Open, an ebullient Trevino accepted congratulations from Arnold Palmer and Jack Nicklaus, whom he would someday join in the top rank of all-time golfing greats. Then he stood on a podium before the cameras and the press, who expected some good quotes. During the tournament, Trevino had quickly established himself as a unique character and a favorite of the galleries. He made such a splash that the sober *New York Times* gave him space not only on the sports page but also

Trevino is made honorary mayor (alcalde in Spanish) of San Antonio, Texas, following his victory in the 1968 U.S. Open. Trevino had caused a stir in Texas with his quip about buying the Alamo (in background), but the residents of San Antonio clearly considered him a hero.

in the editorial column: "Just when the button-down-collar set is threatening to turn the sports scene into a dour stockholders' meeting, along comes Lee Trevino to put the fun back in fun and games."

At the press conference, Trevino lived up to his billing. "Boy, I'm one happy Mexican," he gushed as he clutched the big silver Open trophy. "I'm going to get rich as the Open winner." When asked what he planned to do with all the money he would earn from endorsing golf clubs, clothing, and other products, Trevino shot back, "I might buy the Alamo and give it back to the Mexicans."

That remark naturally caused some controversy in Texas. The Alamo, a fortress in San Antonio captured by the Mexican army after a bloody battle in 1836, is a national monument and a cherished symbol of Texas's statehood. When Trevino traveled to San Antonio a few weeks later to play in the PGA Championship and found himself besieged by questions about his remark, he saw an opportunity to have a little more fun. He took a tour of the Alamo and then issued a full retraction: "Well," he announced, "I'm not going to buy this place. It doesn't have indoor plumbing."

Lee Trevino as a 17-year-old marine recruit. Having grown up largely on his own, Trevino found in the Marine Corps both the discipline he needed and an outlet for his fun-loving personality. "These were guys my own age and we were having a ball," he recalled.

CHAPTER TWO

"What Is Golf?"

Lee Buck Trevino was born in Dallas, Texas, on December 1, 1939, to Juanita Trevino and an unknown father. His given name at birth was simply Lee; only later did he add his childhood nickname, Buck, as a middle name. At the time of Lee's birth, Juanita Trevino was living on a farm near rural Garland, Texas, with her father, Joe Trevino, who made his living as a farmhand. Born in Monterrey, Mexico, the elder Trevino had moved to Texas in search of work when he was a small boy. Like the hundreds of thousands of Mexican immigrants who came before him and the many more who would come after him, the work he found was almost always low paying. During the early years of Lee Trevino's boyhood, his mother and grandfather supported the family by picking cotton and planting and harvesting onions on a farm owned by a family named Tucker. At the age of five, Lee himself began to join in these long and backbreaking jobs.

The Trevinos were very poor. To help stretch the family's tight food budget, Joe Trevino would take his grandson on expeditions into the brush to hunt for rabbits or crawfish to supplement the family's diet of rice, potatoes, and beans. Speaking of those days, Trevino has said that he "never knew what steak was. The closest we ever got to real meat was Texas hash and baloney." The Trevinos were not the poorest of the poor—most of the time, at least, they had work, food, and shelter—but Trevino recalled being very lonely. "I was never around anybody. I was all by myself, no one to talk to. I'd just go hunt rabbits and fish."

As Trevino told the story in his 1982 autobiography, *They Call Me SuperMex*, when he was seven his grandfather moved the family to an outlying district of Dallas, where he had been told he could get a job as a gravedigger at Hillcrest Cemetery. As part of the deal, the family would have the use of a small house nearby. The Trevinos packed up their household and headed off to the big city. Joe Trevino got the job as promised, but the "house" turned out to be a primitive four-room shack with no windows, heat, water, or electricity; the kitchen had only a dirt floor. And the surrounding area was almost as rural as the Tuckers' farm. Later it became a typical North Dallas suburb of large, expensive houses, neat lawns, and sleek shopping malls. But on the day in 1946 when the Trevinos moved in, the neighborhood consisted of the cemetery, a lake, a beautiful stand of cottonwood trees, and grassland where cattle grazed.

Also to be found nearby was a large pasture filled with people hitting little white balls with sticks. The pasture was the Dallas Athletic Club golf course—later the Glen Lakes Country Club— and the strange activity was the sport of golf. As Trevino wrote looking back from the vantage point of 1982, "If somebody had asked me, 'What is golf?' I would have wanted to know when the season was and did they fly fast or did you shoot them on the ground." The first thing young Lee learned about the game was that an enterprising boy could pick up lost golf balls and sell them back to golfers for 10 or 20 cents apiece. The next thing he learned was exactly where in the rough those lost balls tended to collect most often.

His involvement with sports came along just in time for Trevino, and it filled a great void in his life. Well before he had any idea of pursuing golf as a career, it provided him with friends his own age, a little money, and most of all the excitement of competing and winning. He had few other satisfactions. His mother worked as a maid and was away from home most of the day, and his grandfather devoted his spare time largely to drinking beer. ("He was the only man I ever knew," Trevino claimed, "who could sit in a bar from nine in the morning to nine at night, then get up and drive away.") As a result, Lee was often left to his own devices. If he was so uninhibited in later years when it came to enjoying himself, on and off the golf course, it may have been because his childhood was so difficult.

Trevino graduated from shagging stray balls to practicing with a beat-up old 5-iron that somebody had thrown out. He used apples for golf balls and invented putting games around his grandfather's shack. When he was eight years old, Lee became friends with the

Mexican migrant workers picking cotton in a Texas field. Joe Trevino, Lee's grandfather, came to the United States as a young boy and worked in the fields for many years to support his family. Although Lee was proud of his Mexican heritage, he never learned more than a few words of Spanish.

Glen Lakes greenskeeper's son and enjoyed practically unlimited access to the course during off-hours. Soon he landed a job as a caddie, which paid $1.25 per 18 holes.

Lee was a good, hustling caddie. His wages, beefed up by the odd $5 or $10 tip that he earned from some of the well-to-do Dallas businessmen who played at the club, were a significant financial help to his family. And hanging around Glen Lakes with the other caddies was an education in itself. They had all come from poor homes like Trevino, but they were city boys, streetwise and experienced. By the age of 10, Lee had learned from them how to smoke cigarettes, swear, and shoot dice. He had also learned—though only as a spectator—the finer points of knife fighting.

He learned about golf, too. The caddies at Glen Lakes were provided with three small holes of their own behind the caddie shed, and this became a battleground where constant matches were played for quarters. A dozen or so players would take turns, sharing clubs from the same makeshift set. The competition was keen and hard fought; these games provided the only golf instruction that Trevino ever got. As he later remembered, "That's where I learned my killer instinct, playing games with those black caddies and betting everything I had earned that day."

Trevino grew up in this four-room house on the outskirts of Dallas, Texas. The house lacked running water and electricity, but it was located near a golf course: The young Trevino began collecting lost balls to earn pocket money and eventually taught himself the game of golf.

Much to his later regret, Trevino did not learn a great deal in school. The local public school was just a short walk from his home and around the corner from Glen Lakes Country Club, but by the time he was 9 or 10, Trevino was in the habit of skipping school nearly as often as he attended. He certainly was not stupid or lacking in energy or ambition. And there was no question of a language problem; Trevino grew up in an English-speaking household and knew no more than a word or two of Spanish. But he just could not seem to apply himself at school. The main problem was the lack of discipline at home. Both Juanita and Joe Trevino were uneducated and had survived by their wits and hard work; they were no more impressed by a warning from a teacher or a visit from a truant officer than Lee was.

The young Trevino did make an impression on the school's athletic coaches. In his early teens, he had grown to nearly his adult size and was showing all the strength, intelligence, and quick reflexes that are the mark of a natural all-around athlete. Whether the sport was football, swimming, roller-skating, or soccer, Trevino excelled. He was particularly good at baseball, and for a while the national pastime threatened to steal his heart away from his first love, golf. At age 14, however, the decision was made for him. Trevino now had two younger sisters, and the family needed another breadwinner. Juanita Trevino removed her son from school, went to a judge, and got him a work permit. Before he had spent a day in the eighth grade, Lee's school days were over, and for all practical purposes so was his future in organized team sports.

Trevino's search for a job naturally led him to Glen Lakes Country Club, where his old friend's father, the greenskeeper, took him on. Later that same year, a man named Hardy Greenwood sent for Lee and offered him a job. Greenwood was the proprietor of a Dallas driving range called Hardy's. Lee had been to Hardy's once, when he was eight years old, and had left a lasting impression. Greenwood had never forgotten how far the youngster could hit a golf ball, and he was convinced that, with a little guidance, Trevino

could have a promising future as a professional. Trevino accepted
the job. Every morning, Greenwood would pick him up on his way
to the driving range and bring him back home when the workday
was through. Greenwood and his wife came to see themselves as
surrogate parents. As Greenwood later said of this time, "We always
like to say that we raised Lee. We take the credit, the wife and me.
He had the greatest natural swing even back then. He was good at
everything. He picked up balls faster than anybody I ever had here.
He mowed the greens, washed balls, cleaned the range, ran the
shop. I could go out of town and Lee would take better care of the
place than I did. But he was a hardhead, too. He sure has learned."
The stern Greenwood may have been a bit hardheaded himself,
and the relationship went through some extreme ups and downs.
Later on, Trevino was to feel very let down by his surrogate
father.

In the meantime, however, Trevino profited greatly from the
time he spent working at Hardy's. Obviously, he got to hit a lot of
golf balls. He also learned how to build a golf course when Greenwood decided to expand his business to include a 12-acre, 9-hole
course. It took three months for Greenwood, Trevino, and one
other man to complete the job all by themselves. They designed
and laid out the holes; mixed the sand, loam, and peat that made
up the fairways and greens; and seeded and mowed the grass. They
constructed an entire underground irrigation and drainage sys-
tem, and they strung up the floodlights that allowed for nighttime
operation. Thanks to Hardy Greenwood, Trevino also got his first
and—outside of his time in the Marine Corps—only taste of formal
amateur golf competition. Using a set of clubs and a pair of golf
shoes donated by his boss, the 15-year-old Trevino shot a 77 to
qualify for the *Dallas Times Herald* Tournament and made it into the
second round. For all of the time he had spent hitting balls and
playing for quarters, that qualifying round was the first complete 18
holes of golf that Trevino had ever played in his life.

While working for Greenwood six days a week for a period of two years or so, Trevino continued to improve his game. But as he grew toward manhood, distractions such as cars, young women, and nightlife began to compete with work and golf for his attention. Things came to a head when Trevino skipped work one Sunday to play on a friend's baseball team; Greenwood was furious. "Are you going to play golf or are you going to play baseball?" he demanded. "You have to make up your mind." The rebellious 16 year old certainly had not made up his mind, but he was angry enough to walk off the job and—temporarily—out of Hardy Greenwood's life.

This marked the beginning of a dark period for Trevino. Bored, aimless, and confused, he shocked even himself when he stole a set of hubcaps from a member's car at the golf club where he was working. It was the first thing of any significance he had ever stolen. Fortunately, he was caught by a wise policeman who sensed that Trevino was no criminal at heart and, instead of arresting him, arranged for Trevino to return the hubcaps and apologize in person to the owner. Trevino was grateful, but gratitude was no cure for his restlessness. "I was messed up and lost," he later remembered. "I wasn't settled down. I didn't know what I wanted to do. Never had any dates. I'd fall in love with a fence-post."

Trevino sensed that a radical change in his life was necessary. On his 17th birthday he took the U.S. Marine Corps entrance exam, passed, and enlisted immediately. "I had the feeling," he said, "[that] Dallas was the whole damn world and I was going to die without ever seeing anything else except another fairway to cut. So I went."

Next to his grandfather's chance decision to move his family next door to a golf course, joining the marines was probably the best thing that had ever happened to Trevino. He had known several adults who cared about him; he had been exposed to smatterings of education and religion; and he had belonged to a family—but he had never encountered an authority figure in his life that he could not defy or run away from. The Marine Corps gave him this, along with a newfound sense of responsibility and pride. And once he adjusted to the unfamiliar discipline, enforced by a few beatings from boot camp drill instructors, he found that he really enjoyed military life. "It was like camping out," he once said. "I volunteered for everything. These were guys my own age and we were having a ball. . . . I think I learned my sense of humor in the Marines, laughing and raising hell. . . . If I hadn't joined, I know I'd be in prison today."

Trevino's exceptional hand-eye coordination and general athletic ability soon showed itself, even in his official duties. He was assigned to a base in Japan and given a .30-caliber machine gun.

U.S. Marines on maneuvers at Cherry Point, North Carolina. Trevino became an expert machine gunner in the marines, but when his superiors discovered his talent for golf they transferred him to duty in the Far East, where he led the Marine Corps golf team to the armed forces championship.

Trevino was a great shot with any kind of weapon, and he became so adept at the drill of disassembling and reassembling the machine gun that he set a Marine Corps speed record that has not since been broken.

In the marines, he also renewed his acquaintance with golf. He played on courses in Japan and elsewhere in Asia and began to compete in interservice tournaments. At the end of two years, he decided to re-up for another two and requested to be assigned to the Pacific island of Okinawa, which he had visited during his first tour of duty and where he had enjoyed playing on a golf course called Awase Meadows. Trevino's request was granted. His game continued to improve on Okinawa, and his superiors soon noticed. They transferred him to Special Services—in other words, full-time golf. He led the Marine Corps golf team to victory all through the Far East and played in Japan against an army sergeant named Orville Moody, who later joined the PGA Tour, winning the U.S. Open and the World Series of Golf in 1969. After winning the U.S. Open himself, Trevino summed up his Marine Corps career with tongue in cheek: "I didn't do anything but play golf with the colonels. That's when I really learned to play. I started out as a private, but after beating the colonels a few times, I rose to sergeant."

Trevino began to consider seriously the notion of a career in golf. He now knew he could win against tough competition, and for the first time he cast a professional eye on the weaknesses in his game that he would have to attack. "My main trouble in those days," he said, "was that I was a right-to-left player. On some rounds I would hit the most awful-looking hooks you ever saw, and I paid the price for them. I had to do something about my method of hitting the ball, I realized, or I would never become a really sound golfer." When Trevino was discharged from the Marine Corps in 1960, he had $900 in the bank, a tattoo on his arm featuring the name of an old girlfriend, and a purpose in his life—to become the best professional golfer that he could be.

Trevino hits out of trouble during the 1968 PGA Championship. This was a rare view of Trevino, who had made himself into one of golf's most accurate shotmakers. After one of his wins an opponent remarked: "The only time Lee left the fairway was to answer the phone."

CHAPTER THREE

"Let's Play"

When Trevino came out of the marines, he had a clear idea of where he wanted to go in his life but not much of a plan for how to get there. The seven years between 1960, when he was discharged from the service, and 1967, when he scored his first successes on the PGA Tour, were a kind of purgatory for Trevino. In that time he took wrong turns, both in his personal and his professional life. But he kept on learning from each mistake—whether it was a failed marriage or a setback on the golf course—and he kept his eyes fixed firmly on the next step leading to his ultimate goal. "The problem for the majority of people is that they set goals that are too high," Trevino later observed. "They're never able to achieve them, and that becomes demoralizing. I've been lucky. I've set goals for myself that I've been able to reach, and I could go on from there."

What finally saw Trevino through those seven years of ups and downs was his willingness to work hard. This was a quality that, at least in part, he had inherited from his grandfather, who told him, "You want a life, you work for it." Years afterward, when he was an established golf superstar, Trevino's standard advice to young pros was: "The sun's up. Why aren't you playing golf?" Even at those earlier times in his life when he had lost his bearings off the golf course, drinking and partying all night when he should have been home in bed, Trevino never stopped getting up with the sun each morning and going to work on his game. Over the whole period, he hit an average of 1,000 golf balls a day. "There's nothing better for you than hard work," Trevino once said. "If a guy has the fundamentals—a basically good swing—then all he has to do is work on his golf. . . . When I first came up on the tour, in 1967, there

Billy Casper, sinking a putt during a 1967 tournament, was one of the golfers the young Trevino most admired. Trevino felt that Casper was three times as good as he was; he concluded that if he practiced three times as hard, he would eventually reach Casper's level.

was one man in particular I looked up to. That was Billy Casper. He was then in his prime, and he was a wonderful golfer. . . . I watched Billy Casper and I studied him as he hit balls, and I evaluated myself with reference to him. I asked myself, 'I wonder how much better he is than I am.' I concluded that he was three times as good. You know what I said to myself then? I said, 'He may be three times as good, but I'll practice three times as hard, and I'll eventually catch up to him.'"

However, the first thing Trevino did when he returned to Dallas from Okinawa was, by his own admission, to catch up on his drinking. That quickly took care of the $900 he had saved while in the marines, and soon he was once again at loose ends. Within a few months, Hardy Greenwood reentered Trevino's life to offer him a job working nights at his combination driving range and pitch-and-putt course. He would take home a mere $71 a week, but his days would be open for lots and lots of golf. Trevino said yes and soon fell into a daily routine that consisted of playing golf mornings and early afternoons at Tenison Park, a municipal course not far from Hardy's; working for Greenwood from late afternoon to midnight six days a week; and then going out on the town with his golfing buddies from Tenison. Nothing much disturbed the 21-year-old Trevino's routine, not even marriage to a high school senior named Linda or the birth of a son, Ricky. Within two years, Linda Trevino left home with Ricky and filed for divorce, calling her husband a "golf bum."

Clearly, Trevino would have had to plead guilty on that charge, but still he took the loss of his wife and child hard. "When the deputy sheriff served me the [divorce] papers," Trevino later wrote, "I felt like I was being arrested for murder." After moving back into his old childhood home, where his grandfather was still living, Trevino spent the next several months in a wild, unhappy, self-destructive haze. From the autumn of 1963 through the spring of 1964, he kept up a feverish pace, never slowing down and never getting any kind of regular sleep or food; when it was over he had wasted away to 50 pounds less than he had weighed in his days as a lean U.S. marine.

Trevino found an escape from this self-created personal hell when he agreed to go on a blind date with 17-year-old Claudia Fenley, who was a ticket taker at the Capri Movie Theater in downtown Dallas. Soon the two were dating regularly. As Claudia told the story years later, "My family objected to Lee at first. My mother was upset and a little shocked. He threw so much money around on our first date that I thought he was rich. He was almost flat broke. . . . But Lee won them over."

A few months later, on August 24, 1964, with Trevino sporting a brand-new coat and tie and his bride wearing a $186 diamond ring—all bought with the $300 first-prize money that Trevino had won in a Fort Worth tournament the week before—the two were married. It was a spare ceremony without a single guest, performed by a minister whose name Trevino had chosen out of the phone book. The wedding had to be scheduled for a Monday because that

Six-year-old Ricky Trevino keeps his father company during a 1969 practice round. Trevino went through a wild and gloomy time after his 1963 divorce from Ricky's mother, but through all his troubles he maintained his passion for golf and his desire to be a champion.

was Trevino's only day off from Hardy's; it also had to take place in the afternoon because Trevino wanted to get his regular morning golf game in first. Trevino's marriage to Claudia Fenley, whom he would always call by the nickname Clyde, was considerably more successful than his first; it lasted 18 years, until 1982, and produced 3 children—Leslie, Tony, and Troy.

While Trevino struggled to achieve a sense of equilibrium and maturity as a person, he was making much surer progress as a golfer. A major breakthrough occurred when he was playing at Shady Oaks Country Club in Fort Worth and caught a glimpse of fellow Texan Ben Hogan hitting some practice balls toward his caddie. Trevino noticed two things: First, Hogan's shots were unfailingly accurate, each one taking a neat, soft hop into the caddie's hands; and second, the ball always faded from left to right. Hogan was then a few years past the prime of a brilliant career that had started in 1938 and reached its peak in the period from the early 1940s to the early 1950s. He had won two PGA Championships, four U.S. Open titles, the Masters twice, and the British Open once. He has since joined the company of golf's immortals in the PGA Hall of Fame.

Watching and then trying to emulate the great Hogan turned out to be the best kind of medicine for Trevino's golf game. Despite years of trying, he had never conquered a strong tendency to hook the ball off the tee. Herbert Warren Wind, in his book *Following Through*, explains the disadvantage of hitting the ball this way: "When a right-to-left player hits the ball badly and hooks it, the spin on it carries it sharply and fast to the left, and it frequently ends up in heavy rough or even out of bounds, but when a left-to-right player hits the ball badly, it spins in a comparatively soft and slow arc to the right, often stops in the fairway, and rarely causes him much grief."

Trevino returned to the driving range and began to practice ways of achieving a predictable left-to-right movement like Hogan's. After working at it for several months, Trevino found that he was able to start his swing with his body facing the rough on the left side, and his drives would curve right into the middle of the fairway. One practice drill he invented was to swing over and over again, imagining that he was swinging through four balls lined up one behind the other. The purpose of the drill was to make sure he was extending the club well out ahead, which prevented him from rolling his wrists over and hooking the ball. In addition to fading the ball, Trevino's new swing produced a consistently low trajectory. Although he would later play on courses where this would create problems, it was a definite advantage in Texas. "You have to hit them low when you're playing in all that wind," Trevino once explained. "Sandstorms are a way of life in the South West."

The end product of this long rebuilding process was more or less the patented Trevino swing. While it is certainly unorthodox— it has been called all sorts of unkind names over the years, ranging from "a lumberjack going after the nearest redwood" to much worse—Trevino's exotic swing has brought him far greater success than the picture-book technique of countless other professionals.

Ben Hogan, presenting a trophy to a young golfer, was a major inspiration for Trevino. By watching Hogan practice, Trevino learned how to correct the faults in his own swing and keep his drives in the fairway.

After all, the name of the game is striking the ball hard consistently and making the shots when they have to be made, not duplicating a diagram in an instructional manual. As Jack Nicklaus has said, "If there is a weak part in Lee's game, it's probably the flat swing—not being able to hook the ball when he has to. . . . When Trevino isn't hitting it straight, he's in trouble because his flat swing can't get the ball high enough out of the rough. The thing is, I've never seen him when he wasn't hitting it straight. He probably hits more solid shots than anyone out there."

Trevino took his new, improved golf swing back to Tenison Park, a long course featuring many stands of pecan trees, which presented a formidable series of obstacles. Tenison provided a much-needed challenge to Trevino's game, and in later days he gave the threadbare municipal course much of the credit for developing his skills, in particular his putting: "You know what made me into a good putter? It was those terrible greens at Tenison Park and the other public courses I played on. The grass on those greens was always too high, and the surface was bumpy and worm-cast and inconsistent and ragged. When I came out on the tour and looked at the greens, my feeling was: 'How does anyone miss a putt on these things?'"

Tenison was also a friendly place, and there Trevino fell in with a varied crowd of golfers that included poor, aspiring pros such as himself and Lee Elder, rich sports, and a colorful and high-rolling gambling set. The gamblers preferred to play the first five and the final four holes—the part of the course closest to the clubhouse—so as not to risk having their high-stakes contests interrupted by armed robbers who knew that they were carrying ample sums of cash. The golf pro at Tenison Park in those days was Erwin Hardwicke, who remembered seeing the young Trevino "coming through the door with his white tee shirt and his Bermuda shorts and the worst clubs going. . . . He about lived over here. . . . 'Boys,' he'd say, 'We're burning daylight. I got to get back to work. Let's play.' Man could he play."

Stories about Trevino's time at Tenison Park have often painted him as a hustler. A hustler is a player who disguises his skill by using an awkward-looking style or by intentionally losing at first in order to sucker an opponent into playing for greater amounts of money. But Trevino never used such ploys. If he looked scruffy, it was because he had no money. In *The Snake in the Sandtrap* he admitted that he must have made an odd sight on the course in his shorts and T-shirt: "If the mosquitoes were biting, I'd go into the creek and pack mud on my arms and legs to keep them off, something I learned in the Marines. I looked like hell. My golf bag was a little $2.95 canvas job with a hole in the bottom, so I carried it on my shoulder like a rifle or across my back. If I had carried it the usual way all of my clubs would have fallen out the bottom."

Though he did sometimes make bets or play for money, it was never the big money that some of his Tenison friends and acquaintances threw around; the biggest bet he ever won, according to Trevino, was for five dollars. In the words of Arnold Salinas, a fellow golfer who became a lifelong friend: "A hustler he is not now and a hustler he has never been. To hustle is to deceive. Lee was just there with his game and everybody knew it. . . . He made the games hard and forced himself to play his very best."

That is not to say, however, that Trevino was above employing a little gamesmanship or taking advantage of his more unusual skills—such as being able to play left-handed—to win a little money from an eager opponent. The most outrageous example of this is the now legendary Dr. Pepper game. While playing at Hardy's pitch-and-putt course, Trevino began to amuse himself by hitting a golf ball with a 32-ounce Dr. Pepper soda bottle that he had wrapped with tape to prevent the glass from shattering. Soon he had devised a game in which he would toss the ball in the air and swat it fungo-style until he reached the green, and then he would putt by holding the bottle like a croquet mallet. Meanwhile, his opponent would be allowed to play with regular golf clubs. In return for this advantage, a rule of the game was that Trevino would

Trevino shares a kiss with his second wife, Claudia, after winning the 1968 Hawaiian Open. As one of many charitable gestures, Trevino donated $10,000 of his prize money to help the family of Ted Makalena, a fellow golfer who had just been killed in an accident.

be declared the winner of each hole that was tied. Not surprisingly, considering his baseball skills, Trevino became so good at playing the Hardy's course with his taped-up bottle that for several years he defeated nearly everybody he took on, winning hundreds of small bets, before word got around and he ran out of takers. Years later, when Trevino had become a big star on the pro tour, the bottle game paid off for the last time—to the tune of $200,000—when the Dr. Pepper company signed Trevino up to do an ad campaign. He dropped the endorsement, however, when the company started using lighter-weight bottles; he was afraid that young fans would try to hit golf balls with the bottles and be cut by broken glass.

By 1965, Lee Trevino felt that his golf game—that is, the one he played with clubs—was ready to take him on the PGA Tour, where the big money was. And he needed money. His meager salary at Hardy's, even if occasionally augmented by the side bets he won, was barely sufficient to support his wife and baby daughter, Leslie. But in order to qualify for the tour at that time—the requirements have since been relaxed considerably—a player had to put in five years working as a pro. Trevino had already attended PGA Business

School, which was worth one year's credit. All he needed was a simple signature from his employer to verify that Trevino had been employed as a pro for four years.

Hardy Greenwood refused to sign Trevino's application. Many years later, Greenwood explained his side of the story: "Lee just wasn't thinking right to go out on the tour. Physically, he was ready. But [he was] messing around with that drinking. . . . I told my wife, 'We were right to hold Lee back.' Everything seems to have worked out." Trevino and Greenwood eventually settled their differences and resumed their friendship, and in later years Trevino would sometimes concede that his old boss might have had a point. But Trevino certainly did not see it that way at the time. Absolutely furious, he quit Hardy's once again and tried to go over Greenwood's head to officials of the local PGA chapter. In spite of a wealth of testimonials to Trevino from his friends in the golf community, the Dallas PGA refused to do anything. "I didn't get a fair shake, that's all," Trevino told a reporter several years later. "Now there's some of them even take credit for what I've done. I don't hold grudges, but I won't even look at those people anymore."

With her husband out of work, Claudia Trevino took a low-paying clerical job at an insurance company. Having nothing else to do, Lee went back to Tenison Park and played golf. Before long, one of his well-to-do golfing buddies offered to sponsor Trevino in the Texas State Open in return for 40 percent of his winnings. Trevino won the $1,000 first prize, beating Homero Blancas, Gay Brewer, and other established golfers. He and his sponsor then set out on a tour of open tournaments in Mexico, Panama, and Colombia.

Trevino's winnings south of the border barely covered his expenses. But he played well enough to attract the attention of an even wealthier sponsor, a rich cotton farmer from El Paso named Martin Lettunich, who was in the market for an unknown but high-quality golfer he could back in matches against established pros. After a couple of lucrative trips to play for Lettunich, Trevino

Raymond Floyd, a leading professional through four decades, played a one-on-one match with Trevino in El Paso, Texas, during the mid-1960s. Although Floyd was an established golfer and Trevino was only a club player, Trevino won three days in a row.

was offered a job as assistant pro at Horizon Hills Country Club in El Paso, and he accepted. Claudia quit her job, and the Trevino family picked up and headed off to distant West Texas.

Trevino's move to El Paso turned out to be the ticket to the PGA Tour that he had been searching for so long. There, while taking care of the golf carts and the club members' equipment, he continued to refine his game against the best competition available on the sandy, wind-whipped Horizon Hills course. And sometimes the competition was extremely good. In a three-day, one-on-one match, Trevino won a bundle of money for his El Paso friends by defeating established PGA Tour veteran Raymond Floyd. "I can't believe this," Floyd said. "Here I am playing a cart man, a bag-storage man, and I can't beat him."

Meanwhile, friends who believed in Trevino, such as Horizon Hills head pro Bill Eschenbrenner, worked with the New Mexico chapter of the PGA to try to get him the Class A card that would admit him to the tour. In May 1967, they finally succeeded, and Trevino got his precious PGA card. Later that year, he came out of nowhere to finish fifth in the U.S. Open at Baltusrol, and a year after that he won the big one—the 1968 U.S. Open at Oak Hill. Lee Trevino, professional golfer, had finally arrived.

Trevino chips onto the green at Muirfield, in Scotland, during the 1980 British Open. The British Open was one of Trevino's favorite tournaments; by winning the 1971 Open at Birkdale, he became the first golfer in history to win three national titles in a single year.

CHAPTER FOUR

Around the World in 20 Days

The golfers, writers, and other pundits who wondered if Trevino was for real after his 1968 U.S. Open victory soon found their doubts put to rest. From 1968 through 1971, Trevino won 10 major tour events, finished second 8 times and third 11 times; he was named to 2 Ryder Cup teams and competed in 4 World Cup tournaments. (The Ryder Cup competition, held every two years since 1927, matches a team of top U.S. golfers against their counterparts from Europe; the World Cup matches U.S. golfers against teams from countries throughout the world.) Trevino also won the Vardon Trophy, which is given to the golfer with the lowest scoring average on the PGA Tour, in 1970 and 1971. In terms of prize money, he won $132,127 in 1968, $112,418 in 1969, and was top money winner on the tour in 1970 with a total of $157,037. Those were the days when $200,000 was an almost unreachable annual total for a player on the PGA Tour, but in 1971 Trevino's earnings jumped all the way up to $231,224. (In 1990 dollars, this would be equivalent to almost $750,000.)

Trevino's most striking achievement occurred in 1971 when he completed his rocket ride into the ranks of the world golfing elite by winning three national championships in less than three weeks. The streak began on June 21, when Trevino defeated Jack Nicklaus in a playoff to win his second U.S. Open, at Merion Cricket Club in Ardmore, Pennsylvania. Then he celebrated Independence Day by taking the Canadian Open in Montreal, also in a playoff. Amazingly, it was only six days later that he outdueled Lu Liang-huan of Taiwan and won the British Open at Birkdale as well. Previously, only four men—Tommy Armour, Bobby Jones, Ben Hogan, and Gene Sarazen—had ever won two national titles in the same year. Trevino was the first golfer in history to win three, and as of 1991 no one had managed to duplicate his accomplishment.

Going into 1971, Trevino was battling a slump that had lasted nearly a year. But in April he won the Tallahassee Open in Florida with a 273 and followed up with solid play in tournaments in Dallas and Houston. In late May, a smoking Trevino rolled into Memphis, Tennessee, and dominated the field in the Memphis Golf Classic, shooting a 268 to collect the $35,000 first-prize winnings. Larry Ziegler had gone way out in front with a first-round 62, but Trevino's spirits were high. After he sank a birdie putt, the fans in the gallery overheard him saying to himself, "When you're hot, you're hot." They picked up the phrase and chanted it over and over like a mantra as Trevino closed in on and then passed Ziegler. He followed up Memphis with second-place finishes in his next two tournaments. In the six weeks or so preceding the 1971 U.S. Open, Trevino earned two wins and finished within one stroke of victory three times.

Merion, the site of the U.S. Open that year, was a tradition-rich course that had hosted its first Open back in 1934. Unusually short at 6,500 yards, Merion was tougher than many longer courses because of its extra-narrow, tree-lined fairways and unusually high rough. In short, it favored the accuracy, versatility, and intelligence of a golfer such as Trevino over players whose strong point was a high, booming tee shot. The biggest potential problem presented by Merion to Trevino—its small, tricky greens that would usually bedevil a golfer who kept his shots low—was mitigated considerably by a softening rain that had fallen steadily during the previous week.

Trevino started slowly at Merion but recovered on the last 9 holes to shoot a 70 in the first round, putting him in sixth place. He then shot a 72 in the second round to drop 4 strokes off the pace. He remained 4 behind despite a 69 in the third round because a 21-year-old college student named Jim Simons turned in a 65, threatening to accomplish the almost unheard of feat of winning the U.S. Open as an amateur. Jack Nicklaus's 68 put him 2 strokes behind, in second place. Nevertheless, the confidence that Trevino had carried into the Open remained evident in the constant jovial byplay between him and the gallery. Simons had been paired with Trevino in the third round, and he later said that Trevino's jokes and bantering with the fans had taken his mind off the pressure of competition, helping him to do so well.

Trevino blasts out of a sand trap during the 1971 U.S. Open at Merion Cricket Club. Trevino was four strokes off the lead after the first three rounds, but he rallied to finish in a tie with Jack Nicklaus and send the Open into a playoff round.

Paired with Nicklaus in the final round, however, Simons soon faltered, and the tournament came down to the matchup that had begun to seem more and more inevitable—Nicklaus and Trevino. At the end of the 17th hole, Trevino nursed a 1-stroke lead after sinking a difficult putt to make par. Nicklaus was playing just behind, and the packed gallery was tense as Trevino came to the tee on the par-4 18th hole. Waiting for the golfers playing ahead of him to move on, a fidgety Trevino prepared himself for the shot and squinted into the wind; when he was ready, he reached out for his driver.

Unaccountably, his caddie had disappeared. "Where's my club?" Trevino cried. When the terrified caddie reappeared out of the crowd, carrying the bag—he had chosen, out of inexperience, the worst possible time to go looking for a drink of water—the tension of the moment was instantly dispelled by a vintage Trevino line. "I'm doing the playing, and my caddie's choking," he announced, provoking guffaws from the gallery. Then, as if put at ease by the familiar sound of laughter, he got down to business. Trevino drove into the edge of the rough on the left side of the fairway and lashed his approach shot past the green and into the crowd. On his third shot, he chipped the ball eight feet short, uphill of the cup, leaving himself a tough putt but still a decent chance to save par. Parring the hole would force Nicklaus, who had just made par on 17, to birdie 18 in order to tie. But Trevino missed the putt and bogeyed; Nicklaus responded with an anticlimax of his own when, after reaching the 18th green in two strokes, he missed a 12-footer that would have given him the victory. Thus the 1971 U.S. Open championship was to be decided on the following day, in an 18-hole playoff round between Nicklaus and Trevino.

The 1971 U.S. Open playoff is remembered more for Trevino's horseplay than for the golf that was played. As the day began, Trevino expressed a breezy confidence: "I believe the Mex will get Big Jack today," he remarked. But when they reached the first tee, both he and Nicklaus were fighting to control their nerves. Suddenly, Trevino reached into his bag, pulled out a rubber snake, and waved it with mock menace at his opponent; Nicklaus laughed, asked for the snake, and then waved it back. Without knowing all the facts, a number of golfers and golf writers—many of whom already disapproved of Trevino's laughing, wisecracking, and generally enjoying himself while at work—strongly criticized Trevino for this latest antic, calling it an unsportsmanlike attempt to psych out Nicklaus. Embarrassed by the controversy, Trevino vowed, "No more snakes." For his part, Nicklaus shrugged off the incident. "I thought it would relieve the tension," he said. "It relaxed me."

For the first five holes, however, Nicklaus showed little evidence of being relaxed. He landed in bunkers on both the second and third holes, recording a bogey and a double bogey. Trevino himself had shanked a 9-iron into a bunker on the first hole and then two-putted for a bogey. But from then on he settled down and played almost flawless golf, blowing kisses to the crowd and throwing his hat in the air after particularly fine shots. He finished at 68. Three dramatic putts on the back 9—a 25-footer on the slick-as-glass 12th green, a 10-footer on 14, and another 25-footer on 15—put away Nicklaus, who came in 3 strokes back at 71.

Trevino was now U.S. Open champion for the second time, gaining a distinction shared by a handful of golfers that included Nicklaus, Ben Hogan, Bobby Jones, Walter Hagen, and Willie Anderson. (Jones and Anderson were four-time winners.) "Winning this Open means a great deal more to me than winning in 1968 at Oak Hill," Trevino said. "I think it was Walter Hagen who said, 'Any man can win one Open, but it takes a great player to win two.'" From now on, there would be no doubting Trevino's greatness.

Two weeks later, Trevino flew to Richelieu Valley in Montreal to compete in the Canadian Open. He did not play well at all in Round 1, 3-putting a trio of greens on his way to shooting a 73, which he later attributed to a combination of letting down after

Trevino holds the 1971 U.S. Open trophy after defeating Jack Nicklaus in their head-to-head playoff. The victory meant a great deal to Trevino, who quoted the opinion of two-time Open champion Walter Hagen: "Any man can win one Open, but it takes a great player to win two."

the U.S. Open victory and looking ahead to the British Open. A number of big-name golfers, including Nicklaus, had skipped the Canadian tournament in order to concentrate on the British Open, which was set to begin only a week later. If Trevino had not long before made a firm commitment to go to Canada, he would probably have sat out as well.

The next day, however, circumstances conspired to turn Trevino's attitude completely around. First, he shot a 68 in the second round. Then a strong wind blew up in the afternoon, drying out the greens and raising the scores of most of the early leaders. By day's end, Trevino was only four strokes back and working to polish his limited repertoire of jokes in French for the gallery. He pulled to within 2 strokes of the leader, Art Wall, by shooting a course record–tying 67 in the third round and then quickly erased the rest of the difference by hitting a wedge shot 105 yards into the cup for an eagle (2 under par) on the first hole of Round 4. Trevino and Wall were tied after 17, and both missed birdie putts of less than 10 feet on the tough par-4 18th to finish deadlocked at 275. Then Trevino won the tournament with an 18-foot downhill putt on the first hole of the sudden-death playoff. (In the sudden-death format, the first player to win a hole takes first prize.) "I never give up even if I sometimes look like it," he later said in explanation of his sudden resurgence. "I don't go well when everything is running smooth. I have to get mad at myself to get charged up. Show me a man who is calm and he never makes any money." Trevino collected his $30,000 in winnings and hightailed it to the airport to catch a plane to England and the Royal Birkdale course near Southport.

Trevino had never played Merion or Richelieu before his 1971 victories there, but he had played Birkdale and loved it. Lying alongside the turbulent Irish Sea, Birkdale is an extremely demanding course, with fairways flanked by great sand dunes and low scrub and raked over by steady winds—in short, the course was likely to be even more hospitable to Trevino's low, accurate drives than Merion had been. He later said of Birkdale, "Hell, it was Tenison Park without trees."

The 1971 British Open did not feature a great Trevino comeback or a dramatic playoff. In fact, Trevino played with almost perfect consistency for the first 3 rounds of the tournament, shooting a 69, a 70, and another 69. He then proceeded to turn even hotter and built up a commanding five-stroke lead over his nearest rival, Lu Liang-huan. Known to golf fans as Mr. Lu, Lu Liang-huan was an old acquaintance from Trevino's Marine Corps days, when the two had played on Okinawa.

On the final nine holes, however, Trevino managed to make things interesting. His lead dwindled to 3 strokes over Mr. Lu and 4 strokes over the British golfer Tony Jacklin going to the 17th hole, but Trevino kept right on chatting amiably with the fans in the gallery and celebrating with his wife, Claudia, and friend Arnold Salinas, who had been allowed to walk the course with him throughout the tournament. On the par-5 17th, Trevino hit his tee shot into a difficult rough on the left side. Things only got worse from there. He moved the ball only three feet with his second shot and hit his third shot over the fairway and into another rough on the opposite side. Suddenly, Trevino's mind flashed back to the previous year's British Open, when he had aimed an approach shot at the wrong flag in the final round, lost his concentration, and blown a similarly substantial lead. By the time he finished double-bogeying 17 while Mr. Lu made par, Trevino's lead was reduced to 1 stroke. "I really got the shakes then," Trevino said afterward. "I think that was the key hole, and if Lu had managed a birdie to level with me, I don't know if I could have made it on the last hole."

Trevino decided to play the 513-yard, par-5 18th hole aggressively. He reached the green in 2 strokes, thanks to a risky 6-iron shot that flew about 200 yards, landed near the pin, and bounced another 40 feet to the back edge of the green. He made a magnificent putt that came to rest within three feet of the hole, but Mr. Lu had already birdied, forcing Trevino to sink his putt to win. Trevino wasted little time in tapping in the putt and then turned to embrace his wife and friend as the normally reserved British Open crowd—which had been completely won over after three days of

Trevino traded hats with his old friend Lu Liang-huan before posing for this photo during the 1971 British Open. Lu and Trevino had played against one another on Okinawa during Trevino's Marine Corps days; at Birkdale, Trevino edged out Lu and Tony Jacklin for the title.

watching this strangely outgoing American wisecrack, kiss greens in gratitude, and generally bring the fans into the action—erupted in a tremendous roar of applause.

With a score of 278, Trevino had won the 1971 British Open, thereby closing out the greatest 3 weeks by an individual in the history of golf. "It's fantastic," Trevino exulted when asked how it felt to win three national titles in one year. "The odds were all against me after winning the U.S. Open and then the Canadian Open. But I like bucking the odds and this is the title I've always wanted to win. I've never won across the water before."

Now that Trevino was more than halfway toward earning the $1 million he had once vowed to win on the tour, his whole life changed. "I used to tell jokes and nobody laughed," he said. "Now I tell the same jokes and they crack up. Then I had no car; now I have five. I used to live in a two-bed trailer; now I am building a five-bedroom house. I didn't have a phone. Now I have an unlisted number. Boy, that's progress."

However, Trevino's life was not all roses. There were times—especially early on—when his marriage was not on the firmest ground; the problems came in large part from Trevino's impetuousness and general weakness for high living. ("I could give him $15,000," Claudia Trevino told a reporter in 1968, "and he'd blow it in a week. Money means nothing to him.") He also lost his mother, Juanita, and his other functional parent, grandfather Joe Trevino. He buried them both in a pleasant spot next to a goldfish pond in Hillcrest Cemetery, near the site of the house he grew up in and the fields in which he had his first glimpse of the game of golf. Trevino took comfort in the knowledge that his mother and grandfather had lived long enough to see him become a success.

On the golf course and in the mind of the public, Lee Trevino had now attained a kind of superstardom that transcended his sport. Named as golf's 1971 Player of the Year, as well as Man of the Year in all sports by the *Sporting News*, Trevino had fulfilled each of the key criteria for golf immortality. He had won several of the biggest tournaments. He had earned substantial prize money. And the public had fallen in love with his personality, as evidenced by his following of loyal fans who called themselves Lee's Fleas, on the model of Arnie's Army, the adoring crowd that followed Arnold Palmer whenever he played. Adding a distinctive flair to Trevino's popularity was the new nickname he gave himself—SuperMex—and his adoption of a Mexican sombrero as a trademark, which his agent patented around the globe for use on Trevino-endorsed sports clothing and other golf-related products.

Trevino's use of these Mexican themes contained a certain amount of irony. He had been born in the state of Texas into an English-speaking household. His mother had also been born in the United States (there is no way of knowing his father's background), and his grandfather Joe had immigrated from Mexico at the age of seven. Tens of millions of Americans cannot claim roots in the United States going as far back as Trevino's. Nevertheless, Trevino had been slighted, patronized, and excluded from certain places—such as the local public swimming pool he tried to use as a small boy—because of his background and appearance. Even old friends

Trevino clowns with a rubber snake during the 1971 U.S. Open. Many writers and golfers criticized Trevino for pulling the snake out of his bag before his playoff round with Jack Nicklaus. Nicklaus, however, shrugged off the incident, saying that the prank had helped him relax.

from his Dallas days sometimes referred to him as "that Mexican" or "the smartest Mex I ever saw" in a tone that made it clear they considered themselves superior to Mexicans.

Trevino astutely turned this kind of prejudice to his advantage: If people wanted to consider him more Mexican than American, he would play the role to the hilt and laugh all the way to the bank. And considering his liking for the underdog's role on the golf course, the feeling of always being an outsider may have helped Trevino keep his competitive edge. (Dan Jenkins, covering the 1968 U.S. Open for *Sports Illustrated*, noted that Trevino's fans often cheered him on with cries of "Beat the gringos!"—*gringo* being a derisive term used by Mexicans for non-Latin Americans.) At the same time, Trevino always shunned purely ethnic causes, which offended his belief that the individual counts above all in life. Once, after he was approached to help with fund-raising for a Mexican-American hospital, he commented, "Promoters turn me off when they shill for Mexicans as a group. I don't want to segregate. That's exactly backwards." Instead, the object of his many charitable activities is, in Trevino's words, "the poor—black, white, yellow, red—and the youth."

There is also an underlying message in Trevino's famous one-liners and exchanges with the press and the gallery. Like a stand-up comedian telling jokes about his own ethnic group, Trevino often appears to be poking fun at himself, when the real joke is actually on his audience and their feelings of superiority. "Don't call me a Mexican anymore," he said during the same 1968 U.S. Open press conference at which he made the famous Alamo remark. "With all this money, I'm Spanish now." Later at the same event, he quipped, "I almost didn't go up to get my trophy. I didn't know they let Mexicans inside the ropes." And for months after the 1968 U.S. Open, whenever a fan in the gallery congratulated him loudly on a good shot, Trevino would take the opportunity to tweak those who had called him a flash in the pan. "What do you expect from the United States Open champion?" he would ask. "A grounder?"

Trevino helps an intense Jack Nicklaus line up a putt during a 1971 World Cup match against South Africa. Despite their differences in temperament and their hard-fought rivalry, Nicklaus and Trevino liked and respected one another.

CHAPTER FIVE

SuperMex and the Golden Bear

If Arnold Palmer—the first pro golfer to take advantage of the sport's television-induced economic boom and become a multimillionaire—was the dominant figure in golf during the 1960s, the decade of the 1970s belonged equally to Lee Trevino and Jack Nicklaus.

Considering their entire careers, there is no doubt that Nicklaus was the better golfer. In fact, he is widely acknowledged as perhaps the greatest golfer who has ever lived, with 18 major world-class championships to his credit as well as 2 U.S. amateur titles. No other man can match Nicklaus's achievement of winning each of the four major tournaments—the U.S. Open, the PGA Championship, the British Open, and the Masters—three times or more. But in the 1970s, when Lee Trevino was in his prime, he made sure that the question of who was the greatest remained open. For the decade, Nicklaus won the U.S. Open once, the British Open twice, the PGA Championship 3 times and the Masters twice; he won an incredible 38 PGA Tour events, while finishing second 21 times and third 12 times. Trevino lost a large chunk of time to injury but nevertheless won 22 tournaments, finished second 26 times and third 16 times. He won the U.S. Open once, the British Open twice, and the PGA Championship once.

By the mid-1970s, the rivalry between Trevino and Nicklaus took on a distinctly personal coloring. Not that they disliked each other; as different as they were in nearly every way, the two always remained good friends. But a curious pattern began to develop: Nicklaus was the more consistent, more efficient player, and he certainly won more tournaments and more money. When they occupied the same stage, however, Trevino seemed to outshine Nicklaus. Especially if it was a big tournament, and especially if it came down to the two of them, face-to-face, Trevino nearly always found a way to make the shots he needed to get the win.

When asked in a 1980 interview to account for his peculiar mastery over Nicklaus, Trevino replied: "I should begin by saying that Jack and I are good friends. Each of us respects the other's game. I consider myself a very capable shotmaker, but I would never put myself in the same class with Jack Nicklaus as a golfer. During my time in tournament golf, there has been no one else in his class. There are several reasons, I think, why I've done so well when we've met. First, he'd already scaled the heights. He had everything to lose and nothing to gain. I started with a big psychological advantage. I was the underdog. I've always had the underdog image. I enjoy that role."

After Trevino beat Nicklaus in their head-to-head playoff in the 1971 U.S. Open and then dethroned him as British Open champion, Nicklaus came back to edge out Trevino as the top money winner on the PGA Tour. The two golfers next locked horns at the 1972 British Open, which was held at Muirfield in Scotland. Situated along the Firth of Forth, Muirfield is the stately home of the oldest golf club in the world, the Honourable Company of Edinburgh Golfers. The course, which had hosted the first of its many British Opens in 1892, was a personal favorite of Nicklaus's.

Trevino enjoys a laugh during the 1972 British Open at Muirfield. Trevino held off a tremendous final-round charge by Nicklaus to win his second British Open; he also denied Nicklaus a chance to win all four major tournaments—the Grand Slam.

In fact, as Trevino would later remember in his autobiography, "[Nicklaus] was really fired up when we went to Muirfield for the 1972 British Open. I believe Jack felt if he ever was going to score a Grand Slam of the four major championships, he would do it that year because he would play on his favorite courses—Augusta National, Pebble Beach, Muirfield and Oakland Hills, where the PGA was held later that Summer."

As it turned out, Nicklaus was to win the U.S. Open in Pebble Beach and the Masters in Augusta in 1972, but Trevino denied him the British Open title for the second straight year—and in very similar style. After shooting scores of 70 and 71 in the first 2 rounds, Trevino was tied for the lead with Tony Jacklin. In the third round, Jacklin seized the lead on the front nine, but then Trevino came roaring back in typical fashion on the back nine. He birdied 14 by sinking a 25-foot putt and followed that up by birdying the final 4 holes as well, finishing with a score of 66. On the 16th and 18th holes, he gave a vivid demonstration of the meaning of the word *hot.* After landing his tee shot in a bunker on 16, he mishit a wedge shot, sending a low line drive whistling toward the green. The ball should have skipped over the green into the crowd, but instead it hit the flagstick and dropped straight down into the cup for a birdie. On the par-4 18th, Trevino chipped in for his birdie from the rough a good 50 feet from the flag.

As the final day's action began, Trevino held a one-stroke lead over Jacklin. Suddenly, Nicklaus came charging out of the pack, birdying 6 out of the first 11 holes. He briefly took the lead but fell back again behind Trevino and Jacklin, who were now tied. For Trevino, the turning point of the tournament came on the par-5 17th hole. There Jacklin reached the green in three; he missed his putt for birdie but left himself a putt of only about three feet for par. Trevino, on the other hand, fell almost completely apart. First, he hooked his tee shot into a bunker; then, 2 poor shots later, he chipped the ball into the rough on a hill clear on the opposite side of the green, 20 feet past the flag. As Trevino later recalled, his next attempt was "strictly a give-up shot. I was so damned mad. . . . When I walked over there my anger was making me see stars. I had blown the tournament and I knew it." Without bothering to line up his shot or even set his feet, Trevino whacked at the ball with a 9-iron. Unbelievably, the ball headed straight for the pin and scuttled into the cup. After that, it seemed only fitting that Jacklin should deliberately and with great care line up his routine three-foot putt—and miss. Nicklaus shot a 66 in the final round to Trevino's 71, but Trevino was the British Open champion for the second time.

Adding spice to the many battles that Trevino and Nicklaus fought from the late 1960s through the mid-1970s was the total dissimilarity in their styles, personal backgrounds, and approaches to the game. Some of their differences were essentially matters of image; others were very real. Trevino was a poor boy who burst onto the golf scene as if from nowhere at the relatively advanced age of 28. Nicklaus, whose father owned a successful chain of pharmacies, was a child prodigy who had belonged to a suburban Ohio country club and benefited from the expert instruction of the local pro, Jack Grout. He played in the U.S. Amateur Championship—and played well—at the age of 14, won the Ohio State Open at 16, and qualified for the U.S. Open at 17. In 1962, the year that he joined the PGA Tour, he won his first U.S. Open at the age of 21.

As talented as the young Nicklaus was, he was criticized by fellow pros for a lack of finesse. He eventually silenced his detractors with year upon year of winning golf. But although he always hit tremendous drives and putted beautifully, it took Nicklaus many years to improve the other aspects of his game, such as blasting out of bunkers and chipping accurately onto the green. Some doubted that he would ever develop a really fine touch. As Arnold Palmer predicted back in the mid-1960s, "Jack is about at the end of the whippy-wristed stage. He is already beginning to shorten up. In the next couple of years, he is going to find out what golf is like for all the other people." Even when he was playing well in those earlier days, Nicklaus seemed prone to having whole elements of his game collapse. Some observers said that he had trouble maintaining his concentration for an entire tournament.

Under no circumstances could any of these weaknesses be attributed to Lee Trevino, who was once described by a longtime PGA official as "the best shotmaker since Hogan. He is the only guy out there who has every shot and will play them under pressure."

Jack Nicklaus in 1962, his first year on the PGA Tour. Although many people consider Nicklaus the greatest golfer of all time, he was unpopular during his early years. The young Nicklaus's privileged background, pudgy physique, and lack of emotion on the golf course contributed to his poor image.

Nicklaus himself acknowledged that Trevino is unmatched as a tactician. "There are a lot of fine strikers of the ball," he once explained. "Trevino is a fine striker *and* a fine thinker. He knows what he's doing all the time. Where to hit? What to hit? Why?" Trevino's concentration on the course, according to one former fellow pro, belied his image as a clown: "For the twenty seconds that it takes to select a club and make the shot, he's as much a Hogan—a concentrator—as anybody ever was." As for touch, Trevino has said that an important secret to his success is being able to "feel what you're doing with your hands. I just happen to be one of those guys who can feel the golf club throughout the swing—where it's at and the position of the club face."

Jack Nicklaus's public image improved considerably during the 1970s, when fans affectionately nicknamed him the Golden Bear. But when he was young, he was criticized for his personality and even his looks; his somewhat round figure drew the unkind nickname of Ohio Fats. He was resented for being so talented at such a young age and for being able to outplay Arnold Palmer, one of the most beloved and admired athletes in the history of American sports. Nicklaus was painted variously as a soulless technician, a spoiled rich boy, or a natural athlete who lacked a killer instinct and a burning competitive desire. The last words anyone would have used to describe Nicklaus were extroverted, aggressive, or enthusiastic—all words that fit Trevino to a tee. As personalities, Trevino and Nicklaus represented opposite poles of golfing society. Nicklaus was the model of the middle-class, country club–bred professional golfer; Trevino, no matter how many championships he won or how much money he made, always remained, as he put it, "a municipal course kind of guy."

The contrast between the two men is well illustrated by their different experiences at the Masters. The youngest among the four major golf tournaments, the United States Masters Tournament at Augusta, Georgia, has nevertheless been the epitome of golf stuffiness and elitism. Created by Bobby Jones in 1934 and later ruled

over by Augusta National Golf Club chairman Clifford Roberts, the
Masters shares many of the characteristics of an exclusive men's
club or fraternity. The field is restricted to a small number of
golfers, and the organizers waited a scandalously long time before
inviting the first black participant, Lee Elder, in 1975. Former
Masters winners are afforded their own private locker room and
dine together at a special pretournament banquet. Each new winner is given honorary membership in the club, as symbolized by a
ceremony conducted at the conclusion of the tournament: The
previous year's champion helps the new champion slip on a green
blazer bearing the Augusta National insignia. Fittingly, the Masters
trophy is a large silver replica of the Augusta clubhouse, which
looks like the plantation house in *Gone with the Wind.* Even critics of
the Masters acknowledge the beauty of its setting, an elegant and
harmonious landscape of pines, dogwoods, and oaks draped in
Spanish moss. Adding to the mystique, particular areas of the
course have been named for past golf greats, as with the Hogan
Bridge, or after dramatic moments from past tournaments, as in
the Amen Corner, the combination of the 11th, 12th, and 13th
holes, where golfers often resort to prayer.

Many golfers would probably agree with Fuzzy Zoeller, who
once said, "I've never been to heaven, and . . . I guess the Masters is
as close as I'm going to get." But for Trevino, the Masters has always
been a lot closer to the other place. When he made his first trip
there in 1969, the tournament's self-importance rubbed him the
wrong way; finishing 19th in 1969, 33rd in 1973, and 36th in 1974
did nothing to improve his attitude. After he was subjected to a
number of petty slights at his first Masters, Trevino made it a
practice in future tournaments never to enter the clubhouse; he
changed his shoes and cleats in the parking lot with the caddies.
This gesture was meant to be silent; when it became publicized,
he was embarrassed and refused to discuss his reasons. Then he
thumbed his nose at the Masters by refusing its invitations in 1970
and 1971. Trevino caused another miniscandal when he criticized

both the course—which he sincerely thought to be overrated—and the tournament within earshot of a group of reporters. "Be careful, Lee," one of the writers warned, "or Cliff Roberts will turn you into salt."

"Maybe Roberts is god in Georgia," Trevino answered, "but not in El Paso."

On one memorable occasion during the third round of the 1984 Masters tournament, Trevino asked to have the 16th green dried off before he putted. It had been raining all day, and the course was covered with standing water. He knew that the tournament officials were anxious to finish the round so that the final round could be televised nationwide on Sunday, but in his opinion the green was now too soaked to be playable. When the official at the scene ordered him and his partner, George Archer, to putt

Lee Elder, shown here after winning the 1978 Westchester Classic, is one of the few blacks ever to compete on the PGA Tour. Although he was a leading pro throughout the 1970s, officials of the prestigious Masters tournament waited until 1975 before inviting him to play. For this and other reasons, Trevino always disliked the Masters.

anyway, Archer went ahead and three-putted, but Trevino refused. A long, tense standoff ensued. Finally the Masters officials blinked and brought in a crew to clear off the water; the gallery treated Trevino to a rousing ovation. But he wasn't through yet; for the benefit of the television audience, Trevino dragged his club through the grass as he hurried toward the 17th hole, spraying a stream of water into the air behind him. "I don't know what the 16th green is called," Trevino remarked, "but since that day I've felt it should be known as the Mexican Standoff."

For the record, Jack Nicklaus won at Augusta 6 times, twice more than Arnold Palmer and 3 times more than any other golfer in the 54-year history of the event. Trevino possesses two U.S. Open, two British Open, and two PGA titles, but he never won a Masters. He finally conceded that his attitude toward the tournament might have been a factor. "If I'd never said anything about the Masters I probably would have won it years ago," he said.

After the 1972 British Open at Muirfield, the last of the big Trevino-Nicklaus shootouts was the 1974 PGA Championship held at Tanglewood near Winston-Salem, North Carolina. Trevino had arrived a week in advance and had rented a house near the golf course from a Mrs. Mayberry. This arrangement gave him plenty of time to practice and prepare for the tournament while relaxing with his family and a number of friends. Trevino had arrived at Tanglewood in a gloomy mood and buried in a deep slump. He had won only once on the tour all season, and he was determined to redeem himself at the prestigious PGA Championship. His putting was particularly off. Trevino had been searching everywhere for what he thought might be the answer to his problems—an old Wilson putter designed by Arnold Palmer back in the late 1950s but no longer on the market. Then, one day before the start of the tournament, he was poking around the house and happened to find a golf bag that had belonged to Mrs. Mayberry's late husband. There he spotted the elusive Wilson putter, with the original grip that he had wanted. Trevino could not convince his landlady to sell the putter, but she told him that if he won the tournament she would give it to him as a gift. Trevino still owns Mr. Mayberry's putter.

A smallish public course with few really long holes, Tanglewood was an eccentric choice to host a major championship, and the PGA received a lot of complaints from the pros playing in the event. But it was all right with Trevino. The high rough favored the golfer who could keep the ball in the fairway, and rainy weather had softened the greens until they could hold the hottest iron shot. These factors led Trevino to play extremely aggressively. And after shooting a 73, a 66, and a 68 in the first 3 rounds to give him a lead of 1 stroke over Nicklaus, Trevino made up his mind to trust his instincts and not turn cautious in the final round. "What I decided," he said, "was [that] this was the last big one of the year, and I'm the 54-hole leader, and I've got to go out and play with Jack, so I'm going to go for everything. So I just tried to nail every flag, and I did most of them."

During the course of the tournament, Trevino visibly emerged from the emotional funk in which he had spent the past few

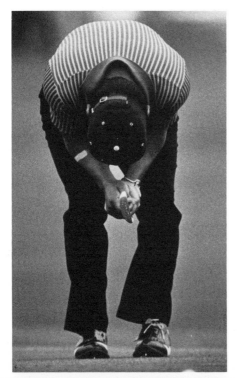

Trevino agonizes after missing a putt during the 1972 Doral Open. Although he frequently found a way to beat Nicklaus when the chips were down, in this case Trevino had to settle for a second-place tie as Nicklaus finished first.

months. Whereas before he had been complaining of feeling tired and saying that he needed more time by himself and away from the grind of life on the tour, by the middle rounds at Tanglewood he was acting like his old self and spouting pearls of wisdom such as: "Ain't nothing like a low round to make you un-tired"; or, on the subject of privacy: "You know what I'd do if I had all the privacy I said I want? After two days I'd go looking for everybody."

Trevino started off the final round with a birdie. Nicklaus bogeyed the third hole but then birdied the fourth and fifth to close the gap to the original one stroke. The situation was nearly as tension filled as the 1971 U.S. Open playoff, and just as he had then, Trevino blew off a little steam by making jokes. For instance, after birdying five, Nicklaus absentmindedly put his putter in Trevino's golf bag. "Hey man," a grinning Trevino shouted, "you're trying to give me a two-shot penalty [the penalty for having too many clubs]. Tell you what, I'll take two if you promise me you won't use that thing the rest of the round." As in 1971, Nicklaus was a good sport about it.

Trevino held a 2-stroke advantage heading into the par-4 17th hole, where he reached the green in 2 but 3-putted. Nicklaus made par to cut the lead to one. On the final hole both men were on the green in 2, with Nicklaus needing to sink a 20-foot putt for a birdie and Trevino an 18-footer. After Nicklaus missed his putt, Trevino put his ball 18 inches from the cup; all he needed to do now was to wait for Nicklaus and Hubert Green, the other golfer in the group, to putt out, tap his ball in, and start celebrating.

But the pressure was getting to Trevino. "I'm choking to death, men," he told Nicklaus and Green. "Do you mind if I go ahead and straighten this thing out?" They nodded, Trevino tapped his ball in for par, and the Golden Bear had finished second again. To Gary Player, there was a sense of inevitability in the outcome of this latest episode in the Trevino-Nicklaus rivalry. "I'll tell you this," he explained, "as straight as Trevino was driving this week, no one was going to beat him at Tanglewood." Not even the great Nicklaus.

Trevino takes a break during the 1975 Atlanta Classic. Only a month after this tournament, Trevino was struck by lightning; although he was back on the tour in three weeks, the long-term effects of the shock had a major impact on his play.

CHAPTER SIX

The 13th Green

The event was the Western Open in June 1975. The situation was a common one on the tour: An isolated rain shower had interrupted second-round play at the Butler National Golf Club in Oak Brook, Illinois, just as Lee Trevino and his playing partner, Jerry Heard, were approaching the green on the 13th hole. Since they heard no thunder, and the rain was not coming down very hard, the two decided to send their caddies out to get some food, stretch out against their golf bags by the shore of a nearby lake, and enjoy a lunch break. Trevino had no idea that he was about to find himself on the receiving end of a major attitude adjustment.

A deafening *crack!* was the first thing Trevino remembered experiencing. Next he was lifted completely off the ground by some unknown force. After a few seconds he flopped back to earth, completely breathless, and passed out. It was a thunderstorm, and its first lightning bolt had struck Trevino.

An eyewitness who had been watching from a nearby gallery said that it looked as though the lightning had skipped along the surface of the lake and then traveled through Trevino's golf bag: "He rolled over a couple of times—I thought he was kidding at first—then yelled: 'I've been hit.'" The massive electrical current had traveled from the bag through Trevino's back, leaving four distinct burn marks on his left shoulder and numbing the entire left side of his body. As he was carried on a stretcher to an ambulance and rushed off to a local hospital, Trevino had no idea how badly he had been hurt. On the outside he was joking—telling his wife that "for the first time in my life, I was six feet two"—but on the inside he was understandably terrified. Scattered over the rest of the course were fellow golfers who were thanking their lucky stars. Jerry Heard suffered a few burns but felt well enough to return to action the next day and finish the tournament. Bobby Nichols was knocked down by lightning but not injured. Arnold Palmer, Tony Jacklin, and Jim Ahern all had clubs fly out of their hands because of electric shocks; Palmer's club traveled 40 yards in the air.

More than a freak occurrence, the whole episode was a million-to-one shot. Even though many professional golfers live in fear of lightning—which is only natural, considering how much time they spend in large, open spaces, frequently holding a metal object—a veteran PGA official at the scene could recall only one other case of lightning striking a pro on the tour, with results not nearly as serious as Trevino's.

Back at the hospital, Trevino spent the next 24 hours in the intensive care unit. The doctors were particularly worried that the electricity might have permanently damaged his heart, but stress tests indicated that his heart was performing normally. He was released, and within three weeks he was back on the job, playing in the 1975 British Open at Carnoustie, Scotland. But Trevino's game was not right, and neither, he was soon to discover, was his health. The immediate problem was that he felt extremely weak; the shock had destroyed the muscle tone everywhere in his body. By early 1976 he had recovered enough of his strength to win the Colonial National Invitational in Fort Worth, Texas, but in June of that year,

Fans try to help Trevino after he was felled by lightning during the second round of the 1975 Western Open. The powerful electric shock numbed his left side and burned his shoulder, but in the hospital Trevino joked about being six-foot-two for the first time in his life.

when Claudia Trevino asked her husband to move a potted plant in their house in El Paso, his back went out without any warning.

The initial pain did not last long, and as far as Trevino could tell, the incident was a simple spasm and nothing to worry about. He was soon to learn differently, however. Trevino's next tournament win would not come for another 14 months. In a pattern familiar to anyone who has suffered from a chronic back condition, Trevino's pain returned again and again, each time growing worse until finally he was unable to swing a golf club. The first doctor he consulted diagnosed the problem as a torn ligament and prescribed rest; but eight weeks later, Trevino could see no improvement. Finally, he saw another doctor who discovered the real culprit: a herniated disc. Trevino has since blamed his back problems directly on being struck by lightning, on the theory that an electric shock can damage the discs that surround and protect each vertebra in the back. Another likely contributing factor may well have been lingering weakness in the muscles surrounding his spine. In any case, he underwent surgery that November for removal of the injured disc. The operation was a success, and after an arduous program of workouts, he was able to resume playing golf.

At times he played very well, but Trevino's back trouble never completely went away. "You wouldn't believe the pain I feel every morning when I wake up, even now," he confessed in 1977. For a period of two years, Trevino followed an exacting regimen of physical exercise. Each morning began with stretching —which included suspending his whole body in a trapezelike apparatus in order to ease the stress on his back—followed by a workout, a hot bath, and a massage. Nevertheless, he would often have been unable to play golf without the aid of painkilling drugs. In 1981, when he had so much pain in his back that he could not lift his own golf bag out of the trunk of his car without help, he was forced to undergo a second back operation, this time for a pinched nerve.

There is no question that Trevino's health problems in the late 1970s prevented him from returning to the dizzying heights he had reached in the early part of the decade. There would never be another 1971. But with a little time and a lot of hard work, Trevino began to rise steadily from the depths of 1976 and 1977, when he won only 2 tournaments and finished in the top 10 a total of only 11 times. Trevino took the first big step on his comeback road when he returned to a familiar scene from his glory days—the Canadian Open.

The 68th Canadian Open was held at Glen Abbey Golf Course in Oakville, Ontario, in late July 1977. Trevino led the field at Oakville throughout most of the first three rounds, in large part thanks to his brilliant chipping and putting. He still had not recovered enough overall body strength to drive well, but once he got within striking distance of the green, he was nearly perfect, completing the tournament's first 36 holes with an economical total of only 26 putts for each round. By the morning of the final day, there was a growing sense of history repeating itself for Trevino. He was playing in a tournament that he had won before, a strong wind was blowing up just in time for the final round action, and he was hot; Trevino's 54-hole score of 206 was 6 shots better than the nearest competitor. And his old nemesis Jack Nicklaus was tied for second with Tom Kite and Ray Floyd, completing the sense that things were back to normal.

However, this was not destined to become another classic Trevino-Nicklaus duel. Nicklaus struggled through the front nine, bogeying three of the first four holes, and as the final round

Although Trevino worked hard to regain his form, his bout with lightning took a toll on both his golf game and his health. He managed to win the Colonial National Invitational in 1976, but soon afterward he suffered a back injury that threatened to end his career.

progressed, it became apparent that neither Kite nor Floyd was prepared to mount any kind of a challenge, either. Their joint collapse gave Trevino an ample comfort zone, which he gladly exploited. He shot a 74 for a final score of 280, 8 under par, and led by 4 strokes at the wire.

Trevino had one other familiar and less comfortable experience on his way to victory in the 1977 Canadian Open—an inability to handle a big lead. He had been in this position before, and he knew what he was supposed to do. As he explained after the tournament, "Nobody was doing anything, so I just aimed at the fat part of the greens." But on the par-5 10th hole, Trevino forgot himself and showed why he always preferred playing the underdog role to that of the front-runner; after a long tee shot put him in temptingly good position, he committed what he later termed the "stupid mistake" of taking a chance on reaching the green in two. His shot sailed far into the rough on the right side of the green, and he ended up bogeying the hole. Similar errors in the past had caused Trevino to lose his concentration and even entire tournaments. But this time his caddie intervened with a sharp pep talk: "Don't fuss about it," the caddie scolded him. "It's history. Now we've got to go after it and hit it again." But no sooner had Trevino responded positively with a 15-foot birdie putt on the next hole than he stumbled again: He bogeyed 13 by overshooting the green and 3-putted on 14 to make another bogey. Moments like these during the final round gave the British pro Peter Oosterhuis fleeting hopes of overtaking Trevino, but in the end he ran out of holes without ever really getting close. Said an emotional Trevino when the final round was over, "When you've been hurt bad, you want to prove that you can win again. And there were times when it came into my mind that I might not win." To this Oosterhuis added, speaking for Trevino's peers on the tour, "In his illness and absence, we've all forgotten how good he is."

Looking back on this period years later, Trevino came to the conclusion that being hit by lightning that strange day at Oak

Brook had been, in fact, a lucky break. Lucky because it made him take stock of himself and realize that he needed to regain a stronger focus on what was really important, both in his personal and professional life. As far as golf was concerned, he realized that he was not as conscientious as he used to be. "I got to the point where I forgot [how to work]," he said. "I got it all too fast. Stardom, recognition, whatever. It went to my head. I was neglecting practice, making excuses, turning into a give-up artist. When I got hit by lightning in 1975 and then had the back surgery in 1976, it gave me almost a whole year to take a good look at myself. I realized that for years I'd been floating away from hard work. I was getting away from the one thing I believed in. Pride in what you do well is what makes a man."

Trevino takes cover during a storm. After the Western Open, he remained understandably nervous about thunder and lightning; eventually, though, he learned to conquer his fear while on the golf course and concentrate on his game.

Trevino's other problem was trying to do too much. His fre-
netic schedule had him making 30 tour appearances a year and
filling in the time between events with promotional appearances,
business meetings, television commercials, parties, and charity
functions. "I've got so much business," he was fond of boasting,
"I'm turning it away." But fellow golfers and even the fans in the
gallery began to notice a change in Trevino's formerly sunny personality. He talked and joked less and was markedly less spon-
taneous and easygoing. After Trevino's 1971 triple play, one friend
and business associate accurately predicted tough times ahead if he
kept up his hectic pace. "He's steadier and more consistent now
[on the course]," the friend said. "But he's going to have to cut
down this year, like Nicklaus. He has so many commitments from
companies and other businesses. It's like Jack says, you're not a
workhorse."

On one occasion in the mid-1970s, Trevino became visibly
peeved when a young girl snuck out of the gallery during the
pretournament practice time and asked him for an autograph. The
old Trevino would have treated this as a golden opportunity to have
a few laughs. This time, though, he summoned a security guard and
said to him in a serious tone, "Man, it's taken me a lot of years to get
inside these ropes." The girl was removed. Later at the same tournament, Trevino angrily walked off the course after a television
crew asked him to wait a few seconds for a commercial to end
before he attempted a short putt so that the action could be
broadcast live. He did not actually show any anger until after he
missed the putt, and some observers thought that he was acting like
a sore loser.

For the major portion of his career on the PGA Tour, Trevino
now realized, his big weakness had been an inability to pace himself. This had led to the slumps, minor injuries, and poor attitude
that characterized many of the intervals between his dramatic
tournament victories in the early to mid-1970s. Talking of this time
in a 1974 interview, Trevino told the story of a tournament a few

years earlier where he had learned a valuable lesson. "I was paired with George Archer at Pebble Beach. I got mad when I missed a six-foot birdie putt and blew up for a 76. Archer was going along six strokes under par when he came up with a double bogey and a triple bogey in succession. But he didn't let it bother him. He kept plugging away and won the tournament big. He taught me something. I threw money away by losing my temper."

Trevino was determined not to let things like that happen again. His punishing pre-1975 schedule had also led to violent personal ups and downs, causing him to neglect his family as well as his long-term interests as a golfer. Now he decided to spend more time at home, cut down on his drinking and partying, and take things easier in general. He vowed to keep his life on a more even keel. When he was feeling frustrated or impatient, he would remind himself that pressure and problems come with the territory, or, as he put it, "You dummy, you could be out there picking up range balls right now!" Both mentally and physically, Trevino was making a comeback.

Trevino clutches his trophy after winning the 1976 Colonial National Invitational, his first tournament victory in his home state of Texas. Despite his persistent back problems, Trevino continued to play winning golf into the 1990s.

CHAPTER SEVEN

"I Could Still Do It"

Now that the 38-year-old Trevino had put his career, his psyche, and his golf game back together, he discovered that there was one last bit of repair work remaining to be done. He was flat broke—or close to it. Years before, he had given power of attorney to his business partners in El Paso and set up a mechanism whereby most of his earnings would go directly into a corporation managed by them. He had assumed ever since that everything was working out fine. Unfortunately, however, Trevino's partners had made a number of poor business decisions, including a commitment to an immense combination golf complex and housing development in New Mexico. In early 1978, the corporation was facing financial disaster. After some prodding from his wife, Claudia, Trevino became suspicious about what was going on but could not get any direct answers from his partners about where his money had been going. He brought in an outside accountant.

What the accountant had to say came as a big shock: Trevino's corporation was making deals, borrowing and investing large sums of money, and paying a lot of people very nice salaries; but even though he had earned millions of dollars over the previous 10 years, there was virtually nothing left that belonged outright to Trevino himself. "I didn't [only] want to make a comeback; I had to make one," Trevino later confessed. "It got to a point where I was scared that everything I'd worked for would be gone. I'd invested badly. . . . I had almost everything tied up in one project and, until I got out of it, it was draining everything. I still had our $300,000 home, but it had a $140,000 mortgage. I had eight antique cars, but that doesn't amount to too much. And I had one piece of commercial property all paid for that was worth maybe $25,000."

It took almost an entire year of financial wrangling—some of it with the Internal Revenue Service, which claimed that Trevino owed a large sum in back taxes—but in the end Trevino successfully dismantled the corporation and disengaged himself from his El Paso partners. When all the dust had settled and the government, the partners, the lawyers, and the bankers had been paid, Claudia Trevino convinced her husband that the only way to put the whole unsavory mess behind them was to move back to Dallas. And so, 12 years after he had gone to El Paso and found the key to the PGA Tour, Trevino's life had now come full circle. He had made the big money, and he had lost it; now he was coming home and starting over.

Fortunately, Trevino came back strong on the golf course in 1978, nearly returning to his form of the early to mid-1970s, and he reclaimed his place among the top golfers on the PGA and world scenes. In spite of his troublesome back and money worries, for the next three years he would play some of the best golf of his life. Most good athletes follow a predictable career pattern whereby they exploit their natural skills and talent to make steady progress, reach a peak, and then go into a steady decline until the time comes to retire. For truly great athletes, however, it is not uncommon to see a rebirth: They make up for the loss of their purely physical skills with professional dedication, hard work, and experience. The result is a sort of athletic Indian summer. With the impressive string of victories that he put together between 1978 and 1980, Trevino proved that he was one of those exceptional athletes, building an airtight case for a prominent place in the history of golf. He also made a lot of money.

Trevino's first and biggest win of the 1978 season came in May at the Colonial National Invitational in Dallas's sister city, Fort Worth. A week earlier in Dallas, Trevino had narrowly lost out to the up-and-coming star Tom Watson, who would go on to lead the tour that year with five tournament victories. And with Watson three strokes back of Trevino after three rounds in Fort Worth, it looked as though another duel might be at hand. But in the final

Trevino poses with the other members of the victorious 1981 U.S. Ryder Cup team. In addition to playing on six Ryder Cup teams during his career, Trevino set records for tournament victories and total earnings that were exceeded only by Jack Nicklaus.

round, Trevino hit his stride and pulled away from Watson, Jerry Heard, and the rest of the field. He chipped in from 40 feet to make birdie on 14 and sank a short putt to birdie the next hole as well. Trevino finished with a score of 66, 4 under par, and a total score of 268, 12 under par, which set a new course record and stood as the best score on the tour for the season.

The win marked the 11th consecutive year that Trevino had collected at least 1 first-place finish on the tour, a streak exceeded in recent golf history only by Jack Nicklaus. The $40,000 first prize brought his total career earnings to $1,754,000 and put him within $30,000 of supplanting Arnold Palmer as golf's second all-time money winner. By the time the 1978 season ended, Trevino had added 5 second-place finishes to his record and brought his total earnings to $228,723, enough to surpass Palmer's total by a wide margin.

In 1979 the 39-year-old Trevino improved his standing even further. The high point of the season was Trevino's triumphant return to Glen Abbey for the 1979 Canadian Open in late June. Again, both Tom Watson and a major professional milestone were involved.

Trevino began the morning of the final day of the tournament in second place, three strokes behind Watson. No one else was close to contention. Nearly every other golfer had been struggling all week on the Glen Abbey course, which had been made brutally difficult by Jack Nicklaus, who had embarked on a lucrative career as a golf course designer. On one hole during second-round play, Tom Kite had watched his majestic, soaring tee shot land within inches of the flag, reverse direction, and then roll all the way back to the front edge of the green. "Great hole, Jack, great hole," Kite was overheard to mutter. Now in the final round, Watson's lead went up in smoke as he took a triple bogey on the third hole, which consisted of one long pond stretching nearly from tee to green. In the seesaw battle that followed, Trevino fell behind twice more, but again Watson squandered the lead. In the end, Trevino's final-round 71 and overall 281 were good enough to clinch the $63,000 first prize by 3 strokes. Trevino was the only man to finish the tournament under par.

Trevino's victory was the 22nd of his career and gave him the distinction of winning 3 Canadian Open titles. It also made him only the second golfer ever to surpass the $2 million mark in career earnings on the PGA Tour. "Yeah, I knew a win would put me past $2 million," commented Trevino, who shied away from tributes as if he feared becoming satisfied with his accomplishments. "Now I'm going for $3 million. There's always a goal, always something else to try for."

The following year, at 40 years of age, Trevino had his last great season on the tour. In addition to his winnings, he was voted the Ben Hogan Award by the Golf Writers of America. The award, given to a golfer who comes back to play well after a serious injury, commemorates Hogan's magnificent comeback from a 1949 auto accident that left him with a broken leg, ankle, pelvis, and shoulder; a year later he won the U.S. Open and went on to garner five more major championships. The year 1980 turned out to be one of the best of Trevino's long career. He won three tour events, a total he had exceeded only in 1971, including the prestigious Tournament Players Championship. He also played well enough at the U.S. Open at Baltusrol to be a contender into the final round. He turned in the lowest stroke average, 69.73, on the PGA Tour since Sam Snead in 1950 and set a new personal record in annual earnings of $385,814, good enough for second place behind Tom Watson.

During his second tour victory in 1980, in the Memphis Golf Classic at the end of June, Trevino not only beat the rest of the field but also conquered the fear of lightning that had been dogging him since the terrible Western Open incident. Trevino, who had won at Memphis in 1971 and 1972, began the final round tied with Miller Barber for the lead. He started off the day playing poorly and lost two strokes to Barber after only seven holes. But then some-

Trevino in action during the 1981 Masters tournament in Augusta, Georgia. The Masters is the only one of the four major titles that Trevino has failed to win, possibly because he convinced himself early in his career that the Augusta National course was not suited to his style of play.

thing much worse happened: A thunderstorm brewed up, and Trevino, who had shown understandable jumpiness where lightning was concerned ever since being hit in 1975, was visibly shaken. When the first lightning bolt struck nearby, he folded both arms over his head and sprinted panic-stricken for the nearest cover. By the time the siren sounded to indicate that play had been suspended, Trevino was already long gone.

Trevino sat quietly in the clubhouse for almost an hour while the tournament officials waited out the rain. By the time the storm passed and the sun reappeared, Trevino found, much to his surprise, that his mind was clear: He could now see what he had been doing wrong over the first seven holes. He walked back onto the course, made a minor technical adjustment, and took command, birdying three of the next four holes. When Barber opened the door by driving into the water on 12 and taking a double bogey, Trevino marched right through. He finished at 69, 3 under par and 16 under for the tournament, and gained a 1-stroke victory over Tom Purtzer, who had passed Barber to take second place. After Memphis, Trevino may not have volunteered for any more picnics in the rain, but he had confidence that he could control his fear of lightning when the outcome of a big tournament was at stake.

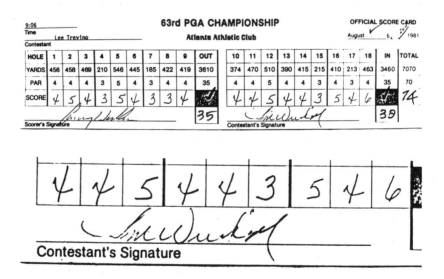

Trevino's scorecard for the first round of the 1981 PGA Championship, bearing the signature of a PGA official rather than his own, is one of the curiosities of his career. Because Trevino had somehow forgotten to sign the card, PGA rules required that he be disqualified from the tournament.

By 1981, Trevino finally began to slow down. He had one brilliant moment that season, during the Tournament of Champions at the La Costa Resort Hotel in Carlsbad, California. He opened the first round with four consecutive birdies, and by the day of the final round he was in first place by a stroke; Raymond Floyd was in second place, and the rest of the field was far behind. Midway through the final round, Trevino and Floyd—who had remained friends ever since their match in El Paso back in the 1960s, when Floyd had been an established player on the tour and Trevino was an obscure assistant pro—were dead even in their quest for the $54,000 winner's share of the purse. The turning point came when Trevino made a 25-foot putt for birdie on the 12th hole and birdied 13 as well for a 2-stroke lead; Floyd settled matters by bogeying 15. But Trevino's victory at La Costa was his only tour win for 1981 and one of his few highlights. On the downside, he failed to survive the qualifying rounds at the Masters, disqualified himself at the PGA Championship by forgetting to sign his scorecard, and finished in the top 10 in only 4 tour events.

As if to confirm the general impression in the golf world that Trevino now belonged to the past, he was elected in 1981 to both the PGA Hall of Fame and the World Golf Hall of Fame. It had been a terrific run for Trevino, especially his age-defying comeback in the years 1978–80. At a time of life when many of his peers were long retired, Trevino had won his fifth Vardon Trophy, played on his fifth and sixth Ryder Cup teams, won five tournaments on the PGA Tour, and finished second seven times. In 1980 alone he outdid his previous personal best in annual earnings by a margin of almost 100 percent. Once Trevino had said, "Every kid dreams of a million dollars. I used to go to the movies and watch those boys in tuxedos and wish to the devil I could do that one day." In the Indian summer of his career, Trevino may have been seen more often in a baseball cap than a top hat, but he had made his second million and thus joined a club that included only himself and Jack Nicklaus as members.

But Trevino was not ready to hang up his spikes or give up hope of returning to peak form. "I can't honestly say that I have the same goals now that I did 10 or 12 years ago," he said in a 1981 interview. "But the number one goal is still the same—to win the big one." Was he serious? Trevino was now almost 2 years on the wrong side of 40. For the sake of comparison, his old rival Nicklaus had won two major tournaments in 1980 but would never again be the dominant player on the tour; he was two months younger than Trevino. In spite of this, Trevino insisted, "I could still do it." And he was right.

Trevino salutes the gallery after finishing the second round of the 1990 U.S. Senior Open. Trevino qualified for the PGA Senior Tour upon reaching his 50th birthday, and during his first full season he completely dominated the competition.

CHAPTER EIGHT

"Why Not Have Some Fun?"

Even after his dismal 1981 and even worse seasons in 1982 and 1983, Trevino insisted that he was far from finished. Considering that he was going to be 44 years old when the 1984 season began, was plagued by an aching back, and had finished in the top 10 only 5 times during the previous 2 years, it is doubtful that he found many believers. But at Shoal Creek in Alabama, where the PGA held the 1984 edition of its annual championship, Trevino showed that he still had at least a week of championship-caliber golf left in him.

This was a far different Trevino from the golfer who was known, for most of his years on the PGA Tour, as a compulsive practicer. Now, after his back had been blasted by lightning, cut open twice by surgeons, and generally abused into a near-arthritic state by three decades of lashing at golf balls, Trevino could play no more than a severely restricted schedule. He reserved most weekends for the far less demanding work of announcing golf tournaments for NBC Sports. Whenever he did manage to play, he made virtually no pretournament preparations beyond a light warm-up. Not everyone felt that this was a disadvantage for Trevino. "Lee has practiced for years and he has the savvy," said the 34-year-old Lanny Wadkins during the tournament. "He practiced more than anyone else when he was able to. And when you are playing well like Lee is this year, you don't want to go out and practice so much you leave your game on the practice tee."

Yet for Lee Trevino fans there was something familiar about the way Trevino approached the 1984 PGA Championship. First, he was coming into the tournament with his old confidence. Earlier that season he had finished second, by only a single stroke, to Fred Couples in the Tournament Players Championship and had won $86,000. Second, he was armed with a brand-new Ping putter that enabled him to putt better than he had in years. Finally, he played aggressively right from the start and attacked the 7,145-yard Shoal Creek course, whose fairways were known for their treacherously high rough.

Trevino tore through the first three rounds, shooting for the flags and recording scores of 69 in the first round, 68 in the second round, and a record-setting 67 in the third round. His score of 204 after 54 holes put him in the lead by 1 stroke over Lanny Wadkins and by 2 strokes over Gary Player. Whereas his competitors, wary of landing in the deep rough, played it safe and used 3-woods, 4-woods, or irons off many of the tees, Trevino used his driver on nearly every hole, going for distance. "At least I try to get closer," he explained with a smile. "Who wants to be in the rough way back there?" As play progressed, Trevino rarely found himself anywhere near the rough. Gary Player said afterward, "The only time Lee left the fairway was to answer the phone."

Trevino's brashness did cause him problems at the very end of the third round. He had been leading Wadkins by 3 strokes heading into 18, where his tee shot found a bunker. Then Trevino got, in his own words, "a little greedy." Using a 6-iron, he attempted to reach the green, but he pulled the shot far to the left and landed in a water hazard. One chip shot and two putts later he had double-bogeyed the hole and squandered two-thirds of his lead. None of this had much effect on Trevino's confidence, though. "That double bogey didn't dampen anything I did today," he said. "What made me really go for it at the 18th hole was that I haven't backed off anything all week. That's the way I'm playing golf now."

Trevino followed through on his words the next day, when he, Wadkins, and Player were matched as a threesome for the final round. Trevino started out by driving into a bunker on the first hole but recovered to make birdie, thanks to a brilliant 60-foot uphill putt. The three golfers remained close until midway through the front nine, when dark clouds rolled into the skies above Shoal Creek, soon followed by Trevino's old friends, thunder and lightning. Coincidentally or not, Trevino then faltered a bit, settling for a bogey and a par on five and six. By the time the rain started to come down hard enough to delay the action, Trevino found himself in a tie with Wadkins.

When the tournament resumed a short time later, Wadkins took a 1-stroke lead on 10, only to fall back into a tie with Trevino on 11. On the next hole, Wadkins handed the lead back to Trevino by 3-putting from 30 feet. From then on, Trevino put on one of his patented stretch runs. On the par-3 16th hole, his tee shot caught a bunker, whereas Wadkins dropped his own shot deftly on the green, only 9 feet from the pin. It looked as though Wadkins was about to gain two strokes and take the lead. But Trevino blasted out of the bunker to within 15 feet of the cup and then sank his putt by the barest of margins—his ball nearly circled the lip before dropping in—to save par. Now Wadkins found himself needing to sink his putt just to stay even. He missed.

After that Wadkins fell apart, and Trevino came in at 69, for an overall score of 273, 15 strokes under par—stretching his margin of

Trevino defied the odds and the experts by winning the 1984 PGA Championship at the age of 44, setting a tournament record. To those who wondered why he had celebrated by kissing his putter, Trevino explained: "I was too old to jump."

victory to 4 strokes. He also established a new PGA Championship record for breaking par. When Trevino sank his final putt of the day and prepared to celebrate his first Big Four tournament win in a decade, he hesitated for a moment. As he told the story in his 1985 book, *The Snake in the Sandtrap,* "Then I thought, 'Now, what do I do?' I was too old to jump. . . . I didn't want to throw my cap in the air, because it wasn't mine. I [had] forgot my own cap that morning and an elderly gentleman in the clubhouse had lent me his." In the end, Trevino decided to give his putter a great big kiss, and that was the photograph that ran in newspapers all over the country the following morning.

Trevino may have been too old to jump, but he was not too old to become the first golfer in the history of the PGA Championship to shoot less than 70 in all 4 rounds. (Sixteen years earlier, he had been the first to accomplish the same feat in the U.S. Open.) The $125,000 first prize gave Trevino slightly over $3 million in career earnings, a milestone that he had mentioned only as a joke just a few years earlier. "Winning this feels great," exulted Trevino in the victor's press conference. "When you're young, you always say it's inevitable that you're going to win. When you're old, the inevitable is over. Mentally, you always feel you can win."

Trevino had recently married for the third time, and he gave much of the credit for his 1984 PGA victory to his new bride. The previous two or three years had been a bleak time in Trevino's life, personally as well as professionally. He and his second wife, Claudia, had drifted apart, and they divorced in 1982. Soon after, Trevino renewed an old acquaintance with a woman he had met years before, when her father was a golf pro in Connecticut. When he married the woman in late 1983, the newspapers noted with much amusement that the latest Mrs. Trevino was also named Claudia. Trevino laughed along with them, claiming that he had married another Claudia to avoid changing the monograms on his sheets and towels. Besides improving his spirits, Trevino's new wife also helped his golf game. She had grown up with the sport, and she

Trevino poses with his third wife, Claudia, during a 1987 tournament. Claudia, the daughter of a golf pro, understood the game and her husband's psychology. When he worried about age diminishing his skills, she told him: "Those clubs don't know how old you are."

understood Trevino well enough to know when he needed a talking-to. As Trevino wrote in 1985, "[In early 1984] I mentioned that maybe my age was a problem out there. Well, she looked me in the eye and said, 'Those clubs don't know how old you are.'"

The 1984 PGA Championship turned out to be Trevino's last big victory on the PGA Tour, and it capped one of the greatest careers in the history of professional golf. He had won 27 tournaments and had placed in the top ten 167 times. From 1968 through

1981, Trevino won at least one tour event each season. He joined Hagen, Jones, and Nicklaus as the only golfers ever to win two or more British Opens and two or more U.S. Opens. He played in five World Cup tournaments, six Ryder Cup events, and was named nonplaying honorary captain of the U.S. Ryder Cup squad in 1985. In spite of his many conspicuous ups and downs, in the end Trevino was remarkably consistent: A 5-time Vardon Trophy winner, year in and year out he was able to record stroke-per-round averages near 70. All things considered, Trevino certainly deserves to be ranked among the top 15 golfers in the history of the sport, and some would place him in the top 5.

Before the 1980s, a golf star's career was over when he retired from the PGA Tour. But this is no longer the case, thanks to an idea hatched by Fred Raphael, who produced the television show "Shell's Wonderful World of Golf" during the 1960s and 1970s. Inspired by major league baseball's popular old-timer games, Raphael wanted to put together a tournament for retired or older golf stars and call it the Legends of Golf. The first tournament was held in Texas in 1978, with Julius Boros, Tommy Bolt, Sam Snead, and other former greats in attendance. The Legends of Golf was a success, and by 1980 it had expanded into a modest 4-event tour, which was given the name PGA Senior Tour—all professional golfers 50 years of age or older were eligible to compete. The Senior Tour developed rapidly, and in 1989 it comprised 42 events and a total of $10 million to $15 million in prize money.

Trevino turned 50 on December 1, 1989, too late to play in a significant portion of the 1989 Senior Tour schedule. But he took the 1990 tour by storm, playing in 26 tournaments and winning 7; to put that accomplishment in perspective, it is worth noting that Peter Thompson, the all-time leader in Senior Tour victories, had a total of 9 wins over the course of his entire senior career. When Trevino was sidelined by back spasms during the first week of 1991, his fellow golfers joked that he had hurt himself hauling away 10 trophies from the Senior Tour's annual awards dinner. Among the honors heaped on Trevino during the dinner, held at the La Costa Resort Hotel, were the Arnold Palmer Award (leading money winner), the Byron Nelson Award (lowest stroke average), the Rookie of the Year Award, and the Player of the Year Award. Trevino was also the first senior player to win more than $1 million in a single season. Remarkably, this was $25,000 more than the total racked up by Greg Norman, the top money winner on the regular PGA Tour.

Trevino is surrounded by some of the 285 underprivileged children he invited to the 1968 PGA Championship as his personal guests. Throughout his career, Trevino has devoted himself to charities that benefit young people of all races, religions, and ethnic backgrounds.

Throughout his long career, Trevino has maintained a deep devotion to his craft. As former pro Frank Beard said, discussing the Trevino of the 1970s, "[He] practices more than any human being I know. The man works." Trevino rarely lost sight of his responsibility to his own talent mainly because he never forgot who he was. "Back home," he reminisced in a 1974 interview, "ten of us would jump on golf carts and play at once in tensomes. The first guy to reach his ball hit it. We'd shout and argue and have some fun. It's all in the mind and the heart. . . . I learned that no one owes you anything. That's what's wrong with the poor people today. They think the world owes them a living. I got news for them. No one owes them a damn thing. You work hard to do your best with what you have. I don't care if I play on a gravel road or on a lake with floating golf balls."

If that statement sounds a little harsh, it comes in part from Trevino's belief that sports celebrity carries with it an obligation to act as a role model for young fans. "Every time Lee talks about winning," a friend of Trevino's once explained, "it is of the hard work it took to get ahead. He is talking to those kids who are living the way he used to, telling them what they must do."

Trevino has also contributed to the welfare of others directly, by donating time and money to charitable causes. Back in 1968, when Trevino was barely earning a living from golf, he used $10,000 of his Hawaiian Open winnings to start a trust fund for the family of Ted Makalena, a friend and fellow golfer who had died in a surfing accident. After the big British Open win at Birkdale in 1971, he donated $4,800 of his $13,200 purse to an orphanage in nearby Formby, England. Immediately after finishing the final round of one tournament in the early 1970s, he drove 50 miles on the spur of the moment to do a benefit for disabled veterans. The list of Trevino's contributions to and involvement with cancer research, children's hospitals, golf scholarships, and other causes is impressively long.

As the biggest crowd pleaser and television star in golf since Arnold Palmer, Trevino made a significant contribution to the sport as a whole. Trevino's time in the spotlight coincided with the greatest economic boom the sport had ever experienced. In the 1960s, the total amount of prize money available annually on the PGA Tour ranged in the low millions. From 1970 to 1979—hardly a time of nationwide economic expansion—the total PGA Tour purse reached the $6 million mark and then shot up to a shade under $13 million. By the early 1980s, golf was the fastest-growing participatory sport in America. In 1982, the *New York Times* reported that Americans had played 487 million rounds of golf during the year, spending $963 million on equipment and $78 million on golf-related travel and lodging—almost double the 1975 figures.

There are no statistics that measure Trevino's appeal to the fans or his unique ability to make them feel a part of the action. His status as one of the most popular golfers of all time owes as much to his tremendous enjoyment of the game as to his many tour victories and one-liners. "My idea of a perfect vacation," he told an interviewer with complete sincerity in 1981—sometime between his 1,000th and 2,000th rounds of golf on the PGA Tour—"is to go to Mexico with some friends and play golf." Trevino possesses a rare power to project to fans the joy and the beauty of play, and he has never let anyone watching him forget the simple truth that golf is a game. "You only live once," he has often said. "Why not have some fun?"

Chronology

1939	Born Lee Trevino on December 1, in Dallas, Texas
1947	Gets caddy job at the Glen Lakes Country Club just outside Dallas
1954	Qualifies for the *Dallas Times Herald* golf tournament at the age of 15 by shooting a 77 in the first 18-hole round of golf he ever played
1956	Joins the United States Marine Corps
1960	Discharged from the Marine Corps, returns to Dallas and turns pro
1962	Marries first wife, Linda; son Ricky is born; Trevino and Linda divorce in 1963
1964	Trevino marries second wife, Claudia; this marriage produces three children: Leslie, Troy, and Tony
1967	Trevino receives PGA card; finishes fifth in U.S. Open at Baltusrol
1968	Wins U.S. Open at Oak Hill

1970	Leads PGA tour in earnings, wins first of five Vardon Trophies
1971	Wins second U.S. Open; also wins Canadian and British opens; named PGA Player of the Year; named Sportsman of the Year by the *Sporting News*
1972–74	Numerous mano-a-mano duels with Jack Nicklaus; bests the Golden Bear in the 1972 British Open and the 1974 PGA Championship; reaches $1 million mark in career earnings
1975	Struck by lightning at Western Open; resulting back injury requires surgery in 1976 and again in 1981
1977	Trevino comes back from spinal surgery to win the Canadian Open
1979	Wins third Canadian Open; passes $2 million mark in career earnings
1980	Wins Tournament Players Championship
1981	Elected to PGA and World Golf halls of fame
1983	Divorces Claudia and marries third wife, who is also named Claudia
1984	Wins second PGA Championship, at Shoal Creek; passes $3 million mark in career earnings
1990	Wins 7 of 26 PGA Senior Tour events; becomes first player on Senior Tour to win $1 million in a single season

Further Reading

Barkow, Al. *Golf's Golden Grind*. San Diego: Harcourt Brace Jovanovich, 1974.

————. *The History of the PGA Tour*. Garden City, NY: Doubleday, 1989.

Boswell, Thomas. *Strokes of Genius*. Garden City, NY: Doubleday, 1987.

Pinner, John. *The History of Golf*. New York: Gallery Books, 1988.

Stirk, David. *Golf: The History of an Obsession*. Los Angeles: Price Stern, 1988.

Trahan, Don. *Golf: Plain and Simple*. Boston: Quinlan Press, 1986.

Trevino, Lee, and Sam Blair. *The Snake in the Sandtrap (and Other Misadventures on the Golf Tour)*. New York: Holt, Rinehart & Winston, 1985.

————. *They Call Me SuperMex*. New York: Random House, 1982.

Wind, Herbert Warren. *Following Through*. New York: Ticknor and Fields, 1985.

Index

THOMAS W. GILBERT holds a degree in classics from Yale University. A former dictionary and textbook editor, he has written *Roberto Clemente* for the Chelsea House series HISPANICS OF ACHIEVEMENT and is the author or coauthor of three other books on baseball. He is a frequent contributor to many New York–area and national publications.

RODOLFO CARDONA is professor of Spanish and comparative literature at Boston University. A renowned scholar, he has written many works of criticism, including *Ramón, a Study of Gómez de la Serna and His Works* and *Visión del esperpento: Teoría y práctica del esperpento en Valle-Inclán.* Born in San José, Costa Rica, he earned his B.A. and M.A. from Louisiana State University and received a Ph.D. from the University of Washington. He has taught at Case Western Reserve University, the University of Pittsburgh, the University of Texas at Austin, the University of New Mexico, and Harvard University.

JAMES COCKCROFT is currently a visiting professor of Latin American and Caribbean studies at the State University of New York at Albany. A three-time Fulbright scholar, he earned a Ph.D. from Stanford University and has taught at the University of Massachusetts, the University of Vermont, and the University of Connecticut. He is the author or coauthor of numerous books on Latin American subjects, including *Neighbors in Turmoil: Latin America, The Hispanic Experience in the United States: Contemporary Issues and Perspectives,* and *Outlaws in the Promised Land: Mexican Immigrant Workers and America's Future.*

PICTURE CREDITS

AP/Wide World Photos: pp. 14, 24, 26, 38, 42, 47, 50, 58, 91, 94, 100, 102; From the exhibition of Hispanic Beginnings of Dallas (1850–1976), Mexican-American Cultural Heritage Center, Dallas Independent School District: p. 31; Original design by Gary Tong: p. 16; Courtesy of Lee Trevino: pp. 28, 32; Reuters/Bettmann Archive: p. 20; UPI/Bettmann Archive: pp. 18, 22, 36, 40, 44, 49, 53, 56, 60, 62, 65, 67, 70, 72, 74, 77, 79, 81, 84, 87, 90, 98